19 vol
180
set of 21

The SS

By the Editors of Time-Life Books

Alexandria, Virginia

TIME
LIFE ®

Time-Life Books Inc.
is a wholly owned subsidiary of

Time Incorporated

FOUNDER: Henry R. Luce 1898-1967
Editor-in-Chief: Jason McManus
Chairman and Chief Executive Officer:
J. Richard Munro
President and Chief Operating Officer:
N. J. Nicholas, Jr.
Editorial Director: Ray Cave
Executive Vice President, Books: Kelso F. Sutton
Vice President, Books: Paul V. McLaughlin

Time-Life Books Inc.

EDITOR: George Constable
Executive Editor: Ellen Phillips
Director of Design: Louis Klein
Director of Editorial Resources: Phyllis K. Wise
Editorial Board: Russell B. Adams, Jr., Dale M.
Brown, Roberta Conlan, Thomas H. Flaherty, Lee
Hassig, Donia Ann Steele, Rosalind Stubenberg
Director of Photography and Research:
John Conrad Weiser
Assistant Director of Editorial Resources:
Elise Ritter Gibson

PRESIDENT: Christopher T. Linen
Chief Operating Officer: John M. Fahey, Jr.
Senior Vice Presidents: Robert M. DeSena,
James L. Mercer, Paul R. Stewart
Vice Presidents: Stephen L. Bair, Ralph J. Cuomo,
Neal Goff, Stephen L. Goldstein, Juanita T. James,
Hallett Johnson III, Carol Kaplan, Susan J.
Maruyama, Robert H. Smith, Joseph J. Ward
Director of Production Services:
Robert J. Passantino

The Cover: SS Major Kurt Meyer shouts orders to his 1st Panzer Reconnaissance Battalion during the 1941 invasion of Greece. Meyer's command was part of the Leibstandarte Adolf Hitler, which originated as Hitler's bodyguard and grew into a Waffen-SS division during World War II.

This volume is one of a series that chronicles the rise and eventual fall of Nazi Germany.

The Third Reich

SERIES DIRECTOR: Thomas H. Flaherty
Series Administrator: Norma E. Shaw
Editorial Staff for *The SS:*
Designer: Raymond Ripper
Picture Editor: Jane Coughran
Text Editor: Henry Woodhead
Senior Writer: Stephen G. Hyslop
Researchers: Helga R. Kohl, Paula York-
Soderlund (principals); Kirk Denkler,
Oobie Gleysteen, Jane A. Martin, Karen Monks,
Philip M. Murphy
Assistant Designers: Alan Pitts, Tina Taylor
Copy Coordinator: Charles J. Hagner
Picture Coordinator: Robert H. Wooldridge
Editorial Assistant: Patricia D. Whiteford

Special Contributors: Ronald H. Bailey, Donal
Kevin Gordon, Thomas A. Lewis, Brian C.
Pohanka, David S. Thomson (text); Thomas S.
Huestis (design); Sally Collins (pictures); Marilyn
Murphy (research); Michael Kalen Smith (index)

Editorial Operations
Copy Chief: Diane Ullius
Production: Celia Beattie
Library: Louise D. Forstall

Correspondents: Elisabeth Kraemer-Singh
(Bonn); Christine Hinze (London); Felix
Rosenthal (Moscow); Maria Vincenza Aloisi
(Paris); Ann Natanson (Rome). Valuable
assistance was also provided by: Pavle Svabic
(Belgrade); Angie Lemmer (Bonn); Leif H. Geiges,
Barbara Gevene Hertz, Laurie Levin (Copen-
hagen); Elizabeth Brown, Christina Lieberman
(New York); Bogdan Turek (Warsaw).

Second printing. Printed in U.S.A.

Published simultaneously in Canada.
School and library distribution by Silver Burdett
Company, Morristown, New Jersey 07960

TIME-LIFE is a trademark of Time Incorporated
U.S.A.

**Library of Congress Cataloging in
Publication Data**
The SS.
   (The Third Reich)
   Bibliography: p.
   Includes index.
   1. Waffen—SS—History. 2. World War,
1939-1945—Germany.   I. Time-Life Books.
II. Series.
D757.85.S74 1989   940.53'43   88-12186
ISBN 0-8094-6950-2
ISBN 0-8094-6951-0 (lib. bdg.)

Other Publications:

VOYAGE THROUGH THE UNIVERSE
THE TIME-LIFE GARDENER'S GUIDE
MYSTERIES OF THE UNKNOWN
TIME FRAME
FIX IT YOURSELF
FITNESS, HEALTH & NUTRITION
SUCCESSFUL PARENTING
HEALTHY HOME COOKING
UNDERSTANDING COMPUTERS
LIBRARY OF NATIONS
THE ENCHANTED WORLD
THE KODAK LIBRARY OF CREATIVE PHOTOGRAPHY
GREAT MEALS IN MINUTES
THE CIVIL WAR
PLANET EARTH
COLLECTOR'S LIBRARY OF THE CIVIL WAR
THE EPIC OF FLIGHT
THE GOOD COOK
WORLD WAR II
HOME REPAIR AND IMPROVEMENT
THE OLD WEST

For information on and a full description of any
of the Time-Life Books series listed above, please
call 1-800-621-7026 or write:
Reader Information
Time-Life Customer Service
P.O. Box C-32068
Richmond, Virginia 23261-2068

General Consultants

Col. John R. Elting, USA (Ret.), former asso-
ciate professor at West Point, has written or
edited some twenty books, including *Swords
around a Throne*, *The Superstrategists*, and
American Army Life, as well as *Battles for
Scandinavia* in the Time-Life Books World
War II series. He was chief consultant to the
Time-Life series, The Civil War.

George H. Stein, distinguished teaching professor of history at the State University of
New York at Binghamton, received his Ph.D.
in history from Columbia University. The author of *The Waffen SS: Hitler's Elite Guard at
War, 1939-1945*, and editor and translator of
Hitler, an anthology, he has also published
numerous articles on modern European history. He served with the United States Air
Force from 1953 to 1957.

Contents

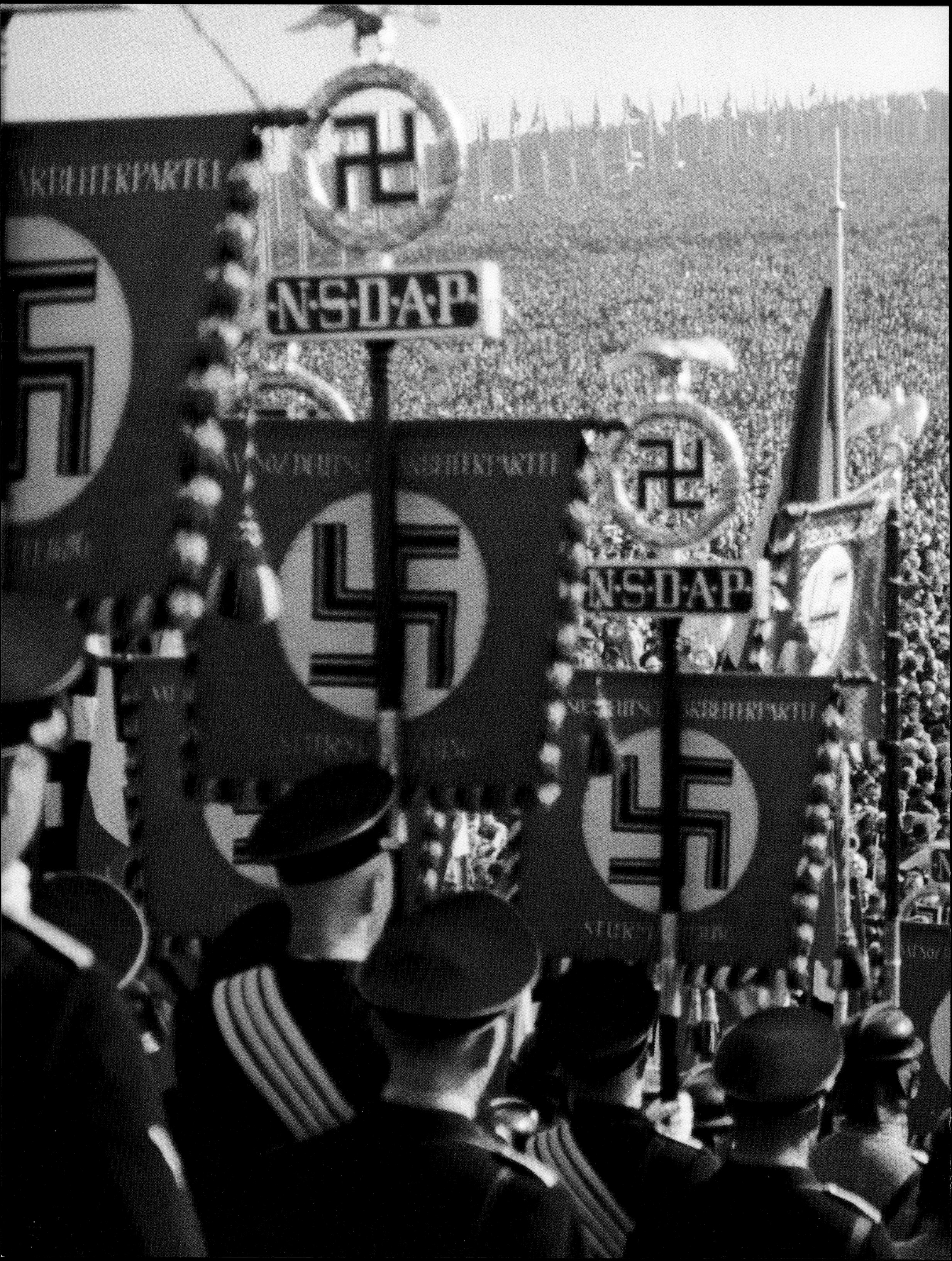
N·S·D·A·P
N·S·D·A·P

Bückeburg, 1937: SS men in black line Hitler's route.

Nuremberg, 1938: Hitler consecrates an SS flag.

SS guards stand alert as thousands salute the Führer.

ONE

"The Future Belongs to Us!"

The young man standing behind the barricade on a rain-chilled November morning in 1923 seemed strangely out of place—more scholar than soldier, and perhaps not even that. He was, in fact, jobless and without prospects. His only employment had been as a novice researcher into the uses of manure for an agricultural chemical firm. Now he stood open-mouthed in a crowd of part-time soldiers, clutching a flagstaff and peering over a barrier of barbed wire at a deadly ring of guns. He and his comrades had gathered in Munich, the capital of Bavaria, to help overthrow its government. But things seemed to have gone wrong.

Heinrich Himmler was anything but an inspiring figure. An awkward, sallow youth of twenty-three, he was regarded as a meddling but generally well-meaning fussbudget who frequently complained of minor illness. His heavy army coat overwhelmed his spare frame, emphasizing the narrow shoulders and thin chest. His pinched face, with its modest mustache and thick round glasses, displayed none of the fervor of a revolutionary. Rather, he wore an air of confusion and anxiety.

Such angst was common in the chaos that reigned in Bavaria that year. Runaway inflation, massive unemployment, and the threat of rebellion had plagued that proud old state—indeed all of Germany—ever since the end of World War I. Now the members of the paramilitary organization to which Himmler belonged had decided to do something about an intolerable situation. As part of a coalition of armed leagues and conservative political groups led by the National Socialist German Workers' party, better known as Nazis, they intended to take over the Bavarian government by force. Then they would march on Berlin and topple the hated Weimar Republic, the moderate, federalist government that they blamed for a disgraceful capitulation to Germany's wartime enemies. They were determined to repudiate the punitive Treaty of Versailles and restore Germany to greatness.

The beginning of the adventure had been grand. On the previous evening, November 8, 1923, they had been called to a Munich beer hall, the Löwenbräukeller, by their leader, Captain Ernst Röhm, and told to prepare for action. They had not been in session long when word came from

Heinrich Himmler, future head of the SS, holds the German imperial war flag amid a cluster of right-wing rebels behind a barricade in Munich on November 9, 1923—the climactic day of a putsch aimed at seizing control of the Bavarian government. When police closed in, the rebels surrendered.

another beer-hall meeting that the leader of the National Socialists, Adolf Hitler, had taken the principals of the government into custody and had assumed power. Captain Röhm later described the immediate reaction of his men: "People lept onto chairs and embraced each other, many were weeping from joy and emotion. 'At last!' Those were the words of relief that burst from every throat."

Then, with Himmler strutting in the van and brandishing the flag of the old, imperial Germany, the group had marched to its assigned objective, the Bavarian headquarters of the German army, or Reichswehr, and had occupied the building and barricaded the streets around it. There had been no need for shooting; Röhm and his men were confident that once the government had fallen, the army would cooperate with the new leaders.

Nevertheless, it had been a long and tense night, punctuated by conflicting reports of the coup's progress. With the morning came cause for real worry; loyalist forces had surrounded the occupied army headquarters with armored cars and riflemen. The loyalists trained their weapons on the sweating rebels but did not at once open fire—after all, men on both sides of the barbed wire had shared the rigors of World War I. For the moment, there was stalemate.

Late that morning, it seemed the balance would tilt in favor of the rebels. The leaders of the coup, at the head of 3,000 followers, marched to relieve Himmler's group. But by then, incompetence and disorganization had doomed the uprising. The officials of the Bavarian government had been released and were working feverishly to put down the revolt. A sudden, intense exchange of gunfire sent Hitler and his cohorts scurrying for cover and snuffed out what would come to be known as the Beer Hall Putsch.

Isolated, the group at army headquarters had no choice but to surrender after two of its number were shot. All told, twenty men on both sides lay dead or mortally wounded. Röhm was arrested, as was Hitler. Young Himmler was not taken so seriously; he and his companions were merely disarmed and sent home. But home—the city of Munich, in Himmler's case—was a changed place. The activist organizations to which he belonged were now banned; the leaders he had followed were in prison. He was without means, without prospects, and very nearly without hope: a mirror image of Germany itself.

During the two decades ahead, both Himmler and his country would find a way out of their morass. Germany regained all its lost power and more, and Himmler grew to be one of the most powerful men in all of Europe. But both would pay a fearful price. An entire nation was about to strike a bargain, much as the legendary Doctor Faustus had done, with the forces

of darkness. The evil genius who set the terms of the compact was Adolf Hitler. But while the leader of the so-called Thousand-Year Reich postured and harangued, the pale, reclusive Heinrich Himmler would be operating nearly unseen in the background, taking care of the details.

Although he never went to war, Himmler came to see himself as a warrior chieftain and would devote himself to the creation of an elite praetorian guard—the Schutzstaffel (protection squad), or SS. Beset throughout his life by real and imagined ailments, he dreamed of a master race of rugged peasants and set about culling the population of his country with the detached efficiency of the agriculturalist he once wanted to be. Shy with strangers, considerate of his elders, polite to a fault, he became the very fountainhead of terror, a man who would dispatch the thugs of his secret police—the Gestapo—to arrest, torture, and kill anyone suspected of being an enemy of Adolf Hitler.

The revival was destined to be a marked success—for a time. But as Germany savored a new prosperity, military strength, world respect, and a sense of purpose, the price mounted. Friends and neighbors disappeared in the night; screams and shots echoed with increasing frequency from SS compounds set up first in German cities, then throughout Europe; sprawling concentration camps appeared like sores on the face of the land.

All the while, the SS expanded in numbers and power to become a sinister state within the German state, inscrutable to outsiders and responsible only to the Führer himself. No aspect of the nation's life could claim immunity from SS interference. Himmler's black-garbed minions not only took charge of the police and the death camps, but extended their baleful influence into science, agriculture, health services, and industry. When war inevitably came again, the elite divisions of the Waffen-, or military, SS marched across Europe alongside the regular army into some of the fiercest combat of World War II. At the same time, Himmler and his praetorian guard inaugurated a reign of calculated slaughter that was almost beyond comprehension.

Such was the shape of the future for young Heinrich Himmler in 1923. His past hinted at none of it. During all the years of his life until then, he seemed an unlikely candidate for involvement in anything out of the ordinary.

Himmler was born in Munich, on October 7, 1900, into comfortable, middle-class circumstances. He was the son of a devoutly Catholic mother and a strict but personable schoolteacher-father. In his youth there was no trace of the sort of dramatic maltreatment—beatings or deprivation—that might account for what he was to become as an adult. But there were portentous shadows. Young Heinrich was forced gently but relentlessly

into a narrow mold by a pedantic father who supervised every detail of the boy's education and every moment of his time—to the point of editing his diary. His mother, formal and distant, concentrated her energies on squeezing pennies from the household budget while insisting that her children learn proper manners.

Professor Himmler had a treasured link with royalty; he had once served as tutor to Prince Heinrich of the Bavarian royal family. The prince retained an affection for his old teacher and had agreed to be Heinrich Himmler's godfather—a boon in Germany's unabashedly monarchist and class-conscious society. The elder Himmler was determined that his son perfect the skills of a courtier, especially the identification and cultivation of his aristocratic betters. The father even made lists of his son's classmates, analyzing their family connections and giving instructions on which boys to befriend, which to ignore.

Heinrich's major disadvantage was his awkward, unhealthy body. At the age of two he fell prey to a severe respiratory infection. His recovery was long and worrisome, and when he started school four years later, in 1906, he suffered another lengthy illness. The years of anxiety about his health left him forever sensitive to the slightest hint of inner discomfort. Through elementary and into secondary school, while ranking at the top of his class academically, he was too clumsy and nearsighted to do as well in sports. Instead of yielding the playing fields to the better-endowed, however, Heinrich substituted tenacity for grace, endured his classmates' mockery, and by dint of great effort achieved modest success in schoolboy games.

By the summer of 1914, Himmler had learned his lessons well. He was a near-perfect student, a conscientious if uninspired diarist, a churchgoer, and pianist. His leisure time was structured and supervised; he went hiking and swimming with the family (or bicycle riding with his elder brother, Gebhard, enduring frequent falls) and collected stamps, coins, and medieval artifacts, exactly as his father had always done. In his diary he reproached himself for the slightest lapse from his rigorous routine, for his clumsiness, and for talking too much. At the same time he expressed contempt for those less disciplined than himself.

At that time, the family was living in Landshut, forty miles northeast of Munich, where the senior Himmler had taken a job as deputy principal of the secondary school. It had been a welcome advance in his career, and the family had a number of friends living in the area; life was outwardly settled and pleasant. Then, on July 29, an underlined phrase appeared in Heinrich's diary: Beginning of war between Austria and Serbia. Himmler followed the events of the escalating conflict with a schoolboy's fervor, but until 1917 he was too young to participate in anything other than relief

Munich, viewed along a downtown thoroughfare in 1925, was the bustling capital of Bavaria and a bastion of antirepublicanism. In the chaotic aftermath of World War I, a communist uprising in the city was crushed by ultraconservative army veterans, paving the way for the emergence of the Nazis.

Glimpses of a Homespun Himmler

Heinrich (*left*) flanks brother Gebhard in 1918.

A skirted Heinrich fronts a family portrait, circa 1902.

The SS chief earns his sports badge in the 1930s.

Himmler poses with his estranged wife Margarete in 1936.

The Bavarian squire takes target practice in 1935.

Belying his grim reputation, the Reichsführer-SS embraces his beloved daughter Gudrun at a 1938 sports festival.

work and home guard training. After he turned seventeen—old enough for wartime military service—his father managed to arrange an appointment to an officers' training program. (It was unthinkable that Heinrich should enlist as a common soldier.)

In the first days of January 1918, the young man finally reported for training as an officer candidate in the Eleventh Bavarian Infantry Regiment. The sudden separation from home and family caused him considerable shock, but he was determined to succeed. With the same grim tenacity he had applied to school sports, he endured cold rooms, common showers, army food, and physical exertion. He complained constantly to his parents, but he made it through. By October he had passed basic training, a cadet course, and machine-gun school. But to Himmler's everlasting frustration, the war ended just as he finished his training. Later he would claim that he had led men in combat, but marching a few trainees around a parade ground was as close as he got to the Great War.

Crestfallen, Himmler returned home to find that, almost overnight, everything had changed. The family's patron, Prince Heinrich, had been killed in action. The monarchy itself was a casualty; prostrated by the lost war, threatened with revolution, Germany had turned itself into a democratic republic. The aristocrats, whose cultivation had been the Himmler family's main avocation, were stripped of power.

From the beginning, the Weimar government seemed impotent. Among other failures, it could not stem the inflation that was consuming the purchasing power and savings of all Germans. When Himmler enrolled in the technical college in Munich as an agricultural student in 1919, his father was increasingly hard-pressed to pay his expenses. For a time it looked as though Himmler would have to drop out. With unemployment rampant, his prospects were uncertain even with a diploma; without one, they would be nonexistent.

Despite the worries, Himmler entered undergraduate life with enthusiasm, joining a fraternity and acquiring the requisite dueling scars. Fending off another bout with illness, he graduated in 1922 with a degree in agriculture. He hoped for a commission in the army, but the Reichswehr's postwar size was restricted by the Versailles treaty, and competition was too stiff. At length he landed a modest job—as a technical assistant with a nitrogen fertilizer company—only to see his salary lose half its value to inflation in a single month.

The worse things became, the more Himmler was attracted by the corrosive, hate-filled railings of the right wing. All over Germany, frenzied little political clubs had organized to identify scapegoats and to tout solutions for the country's worsening problems. Many of these groups were

made up of angry, disillusioned former soldiers who had been not only humiliated but deprived of employment by the capitulation at Versailles. Himmler, who liked to think of himself as a veteran officer, identified with their point of view and quit his job to be with them. He soon found among them a man who promised action.

Ernst Röhm was a literally battle-scarred professional soldier with no interest in any other livelihood; he was a squat, red-faced, hard-eyed man who radiated all the grace and subtlety of a tank. With his combat ribbons and ramrod attitude, he seemed everything Himmler wanted to become. Assisted by his former army superiors, Röhm had been struggling since the end of the war to preserve some military strength in the ruins of Germany's defeat. He had secreted in various places around Bavaria large caches of contraband weapons and ammunition. He also had organized underground army regiments in defiance of the Versailles treaty, and when they were banned by the nervous Weimar government, he reorganized them as a national militia, which was in turn disbanded. Still Röhm persisted, holding together a federation of small, right-wing paramilitary organizations. Himmler, the frustrated army veteran, joined several of these groups.

Röhm had become an agent for some of the most powerful people in Germany, who were determined as he was to restore the might of the army and of Germany itself. While he felt eminently qualified in military matters, he realized that his task would require popular appeal, which he completely lacked. For political success he needed a frontman who could beguile the masses while soldiers did the real work. Röhm had identified such a man in Adolf Hitler, the impassioned leader of the puny Nazi party. An admiring Himmler followed in Röhm's wake, joining the National Socialists in August of 1923, just before resentment of the Weimar government came to a head.

Threatened on every side, the government declared a state of emergency and gave dictatorial powers to the army. Bavaria, in an increasingly separatist mood, refused to obey directives from Berlin. But Röhm and the National Socialists did not want to leave the republic; they wanted to destroy it. "Down with the November criminals!" they chanted, cursing the "traitors of the fatherland" who had agreed to the hated Versailles treaty. Together they mounted the brief revolt that Germans would remember as the Beer Hall Putsch.

After the debacle in Munich, Himmler found his life and his country sliding deeper into malaise. He searched for a job in Bavaria, Turkey, Italy, and even the Ukraine. Soviet Russia was an unlikely place for Himmler to

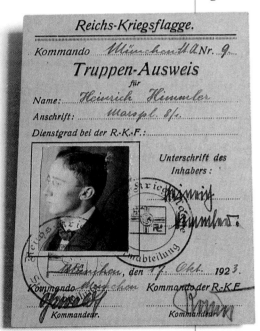

Shortly before the Beer Hall Putsch, this identification card was issued to Himmler by the paramilitary organization Reichskriegsflagge (RKF), named for the imperial war flag shown on the validating stamp. The swastika signals the RKF's association with the Nazi party.

consider making a fresh start, given his loathing of communism, but he was in the grip of a number of paradoxical beliefs. In many respects, his thoughts were an unremarkable jumble of sophomoric conclusions about the way of the world, but they were given a frantic edge by the need to explain—or at least to assign blame for—the doldrums in which he found himself. Only the angry rhetoric of the Nazi party, with its twin pillars of ultranationalism and anti-Semitism, satisfied that need. The party was banned after the attempted coup, but it simply split into two factions with different names, one of which was run by a pharmacist named Gregor Strasser. Himmler soon became a fervent party activist, traveling around southern Bavaria throughout 1924 delivering speeches such as "The Enslavement of the Workers by Stock Exchange Capitalists." He became a thoroughly committed revolutionary. "We few do this hard work undeterred," he wrote. "It is a selfless service to a great idea and a great cause."

The party's virulent message was attractive not only to Himmler, but to an electorate that was fully as frightened and confused as he was. In the elections that May, both Strasser and Röhm—who had just been released from prison—won seats in the Reichstag, Germany's national parliament. Himmler, as a reward for his services, was appointed secretary to Strasser. "The fellow's doubly useful," said Strasser with some disdain. "He's got a motorbike, and he's full of frustrated ambition to be a soldier."

Himmler's new job was in Landshut, his former hometown. He threw

The men of Hitler's personal *Stosstrupp*, or assault squad, embark for a rally in September 1923. Assigned to guard Hitler and bully his opponents, these forerunners of the SS wore army-style jackets and death's-heads on their caps to distinguish themselves from the brown-shirted Storm Troopers.

himself into his work with redoubled energy, but new elections held in December of 1924 brought disaster. Although Strasser managed to retain his seat in the Reichstag, Röhm was defeated, and the fortunes of Strasser's party reached a low ebb. Then, on December 20, Hitler was released from prison, and shortly thereafter the ban on the Nazi party was lifted by an overconfident state government. "The wild beast is checked," declared the Bavarian prime minister, Heinrich Held, in a monumental miscalculation. "We can afford to loosen the chain."

Early in 1925 Strasser obediently led his followers back into the Nazi fold. He expected Hitler to reach out to other like-minded parties in order to form a more potent coalition. But the Hitler who emerged from prison was even more intractable than the one who had led the putsch. There would

SA chieftain Ernst Röhm displays his scars and medals from World War I. Röhm never lost his lust for battle, boasting that "war and unrest appeal to me more than the good bourgeois order."

be no cooperation with any other organization; the price of association with the Nazis was to be absolute, unquestioning subservience to Hitler. And there would be no more attempted coups; the road to power was to be the long one of legal electioneering. These new, inflexible policies led to serious friction between Hitler and his top subordinates.

The most serious rift was with Röhm. Four years earlier, the aggressive captain had helped organize a gang of roughnecks to keep order at party meetings and protect party leaders. Before long this brown-shirted auxiliary, the Sturmabteilung (SA), or Storm Troopers, had gone on the offensive against other political parties, breaking into their meeting halls, beating their leaders, and chasing their members through the streets. Hitler had urged them on, vowing openly to disrupt "all meetings or lectures that are likely to distract the minds of our fellow countrymen." Röhm's former soldiers and hard cases had performed this task with such unreserved vigor that in 1925 there was great reluctance in some state governments to let the SA be reconstituted along with the Nazi party.

Moreover, Röhm was a prickly subordinate. In fact, he did not regard himself as a subordinate at all. "I categorically refuse to allow the SA to become involved in party matters," he told Hitler; "equally, I categorically refuse to allow SA commanders to accept instructions from party political leaders." It was he who had the power, Röhm believed, and Hitler who should take orders. To make matters worse, Röhm was a brazenly promiscuous homosexual who used his position of power to recruit men and boys for nightly excursions into debauchery. Predictably, in January of 1925 his assignations involved him in a lurid scandal that made him the object of widespread contempt. Under

intense pressure from Hitler and disgusted both by the Nazi party's new commitment to legality and by its wariness of strong-arm tactics, Röhm resigned and went to Bolivia.

There was also trouble between Hitler and Gregor Strasser, now leader of the Nazi party in northern Germany. Strasser and his brother Otto, editor of the National Socialist newspaper in Berlin, disagreed strongly with Hitler's economic policy; they still took seriously the word *socialist* in the party's official title, while Hitler was more interested in appealing to the wealthy industrialists whose financial support he craved.

Meanwhile, Himmler toiled happily on at a variety of party jobs, affected neither by the troubles of his chief mentors nor by the profound distaste of his family for his new life as a radical politician. Himmler, the indefatigable diarist, the arranger of the minutiae of life, had found the perfect outlet for his compulsive scheduling and bookkeeping, and for his lifelong training in the art of currying favor with his superiors. The harsher Hitler sounded and the more dismal the party's prospects seemed, the harder Himmler worked and the more fanatical he became. He pronounced Hitler the "greatest brain of all times" and clicked his heels at the sound of the leader's voice on the telephone. And if one of Himmler's colleagues is to be believed, while he worked at his desk he conversed respectfully with Hitler's picture on the wall. Himmler's reward was not long in coming.

Hitler wanted a reliable security force of his own, one that could both operate where the SA was banned and dilute the power of the remaining SA units. Around a nucleus of former personal bodyguards, he created the Schutzstaffel, or SS. Its members were to be "men who were ready for revolution, and knew that someday things would come to hard knocks." Loyalty was more important than numbers; twenty men to a city would be enough, "on condition that one could count on them absolutely." There would be no more of Röhm's excesses; "habitual drunkards, gossipmongers, and other delinquents will not be considered."

Himmler met all the requirements of the new cadre and was the natural choice to organize the SS unit in southern Bavaria. But despite its elite status and distinctive regalia—black caps with silver death's-head buttons and black-bordered swastika armbands—the SS at first attracted few recruits, and those few had little to do. They were reduced to such tasks as selling subscriptions to the party newspaper. The problem was that the German economy at last was beginning to improve. Unemployment was down, production was up, the country was being rebuilt, and few had time to listen to Hitler's feverish rantings. That the prosperity was temporary, based on enormous loans that would one day come due with disastrous consequences, almost no one realized at the time.

Hitler prepares to review 30,000 Storm Troopers at the first Party Day rally at Nuremberg in 1927. Himmler, now an SS commander, stands by a banner that reads, "Germany, awake!" Behind Himmler are Hitler's secretary, Rudolf Hess, and to Hess's left, ideologue Gregor Strasser.

Himmler persevered nevertheless, ever more strident about the nobility of the German peasant and the venality of capitalists and Jews. By 1925 he was judging writers, speakers, and acquaintances according to whether they were hard or soft on what he called the "Jewish question." He announced a plan to publish, as a public service, "the names of all Jews, as well as of all Christian friends of the Jews, residing in Lower Bavaria." When Gregor Strasser learned of the project, he laughed and observed that Himmler was becoming a fanatic.

Despite Strasser's disagreements with Hitler, the pharmacist was a brilliant recruiter, and Hitler needed nothing so much as more followers. In 1926 Strasser was promoted to party propaganda chief, a job that required moving to Munich, and he took Himmler along as his deputy. Strasser still did not regard Himmler as any kind of leader. When a further move to Berlin was in the offing, Strasser said of his assistant, "He's very ambitious, but I won't take him along north—he's no worldbeater, you know."

Strasser could be dismissive about Himmler but could not dismiss him; the deputy was simply too diligent and useful to be set aside. He kept order, promoted stability, and as much as anyone in this arid period, contributed to a slow but steady growth in the membership of the party—and the SS. Before long he was traveling to Berlin, as well as other places, on party business. During one such trip, Himmler ran from a rainstorm into a hotel lobby and found himself face-to-face with a large, blond, Germanic beauty. Attempting a gallant gesture, he swept off his hat, spattering the young woman with a cold shower. Nevertheless, they began to talk. She was Margarete Boden, a former army nurse and owner of a clinic specializing in herbal and homeopathic medicine. She proved to be his equal in fussiness and frugality, and their mutual interests in peasantry, agriculture, and inflexible routine soon drew them together. The romance caused more difficulty between Himmler and his parents; the woman was eight years his senior, Protestant, and divorced. But Himmler was adamant, and they were married in July of 1928.

Margarete sold her clinic, and with the proceeds the couple bought a small farm at Waldtrudering, ten miles from Munich. After years of wanting to manage a farm and have his own domestic life, Himmler made an enthusiastic start on the new venture. The couple raised and sold produce, dealt in farm implements, and kept fifty laying hens. They even made a small profit, and in 1929 their daughter Gudrun was born.

At the same time, Himmler's six years of toil on behalf of the Nazi party began to pay off in a way that assured he would spend little more time at the farm. On January 6, 1929, Hitler appointed him Reichsführer, or national commander, of the SS. Despite the grand title, it was not an especially powerful post. The organization had fewer than 300 members; there was an independent SS commander in Berlin, Kurt Daluege, whose relationship to Himmler was unclear; and overall authority for the Nazi paramilitary forces was still vested in the SA. But the promotion confirmed Himmler in his obsessive approach to work and offered free rein to his poisonous beliefs about race. Methodically, with little outward demonstration but with great intensity, he went to work.

At first it did not go smoothly. Himmler decreed that no one would be admitted to the SS who did not display the outward signs of Nordic, or so-called Aryan, ancestry: The men under his command should be tall, blue-eyed, and fair. But since a large proportion of his existing membership failed even this initial test, he made exception for World War I veterans. He imposed a requirement for a candidate's minimum height, but it was a mere five feet eight inches. For the time being, the main test of an applicant was a lengthy examination of his photograph by Himmler himself, wielding

Germany in 1930 (red border) had shrunk from its pre-World War I boundaries (broken lines), a result of territorial concessions (dark green) forced on the country at Versailles by the Allies. Hitler and his followers castigated the leaders of the Weimar Republic for accepting such affronts to national pride as the Polish Corridor, which severed East Prussia from the rest of Germany. Political turmoil was exacerbated by the weakness of the central government: Germany comprised eighteen states, each with a tradition of independence.

In 1931 Himmler *(in glasses)* and racial theorist Walther Darré *(at Himmler's left)* commune with spirit among Bavarian farmers gathered beneath Hitler's portrait. Himmler's SS cultivated a following among farmers, whom Darré called the "life source of the Nordic race."

a magnifying glass and brooding. "I used to think: Are there any definite indications of foreign blood in this man—prominent cheek bones, for instance—that might cause people to say, 'He has a Mongolian or Slav look about him'?" The ultimate aim, he explained, was to create "an order of good blood to serve Germany." This was to be no mere bodyguard or security force. Whether it was clear at the time or simply a set of muddled impulses to be defined later, Himmler was laying the foundations of a master race whose destiny was to assume all the powers of the German state and then of the world.

The idea that the Germanic race had been somehow endowed with an inherent superiority, contrasting with the malignancies of such strains as the Slavs, Latins, and Jews, had enjoyed currency in Germany since the nineteenth century. A corollary held that a stronger race, or nation, had a natural right to dominate or even exterminate weaker nations in the general struggle for survival. Various versions of the message, often buttressed by claims of scientific research, appeared over the years to fester in the German consciousness.

One of the latter-day proponents of the racial ideology was Alfred Rosenberg. Born of German parents in the Russian province of Estonia and educated in Moscow, Rosenberg fled to Munich during the Russian Revolution, bringing with him a profound hatred of both Bolsheviks and Jews. Hitler thought him an intellectual, and in 1923 made him editor of the Nazi newspaper, *Völkischer Beobachter.*

Rosenberg denounced indiscriminantly Jews, Freemasons, communists, and Christians. He proposed a new religion that would oppose the weak doctrine of Christian love with a strong ideal of racial superiority. "A culture always decays," he wrote, "when humanitarian ideals obstruct the right of the dominant race to rule those it has subjugated." His "new faith," as he attempted to explain it, was "the belief, incarnate with the most lucid knowledge, that Nordic blood represents that mystery which has replaced and overcome the old sacraments." With such impenetrable bunk, Rosenberg became recognized as the preeminent Nazi philosopher. Even Hitler, his sponsor, called Rosenberg's writing "illogical rubbish." Joseph Goebbels, the future propaganda chieftain, dismissed it as an "ideological belch." And although more than a million copies of the Nazi philosopher's masterpiece, *The Myth of the Twentieth Century*, were sold, few people could be found later who had actually read it.

One who did read and admire Rosenberg's theories was Walther Darré, an English-educated Argentinian of German parentage whose area of expertise was agriculture and whose consuming enthusiasm was the peasantry. He shared Rosenberg's vision of the man of the future as a "powerful, earthbound figure," a "strong peasant" willing to impose his natural Nordic superiority on any inferior. In 1929, the year Himmler took over the SS, Darré published a treatise titled *Blood and Soil*, extolling the virtues of Nordic peasants—who were especially graced, he wrote, if they were raised on soil of a certain composition. He called for an energetic program of selective breeding to ensure their expansion and gradual domination of such decadent bloodlines as those of the Jews and Slavs. Himmler loved the book, befriended its author, and soon brought Darré into the SS to pursue his research with official sanction.

With the help of his theoretician, Himmler found innocuous, agricultural metaphors with which to cloak the horror of what he was contemplating: "We are like the plant-breeding specialist who, when he wants to breed a pure new strain, first goes over the field to cull the unwanted plants. We, too, shall begin by weeding out the people who, in our opinion, are not suitable SS material." The work absorbed Himmler completely; his farm and wife were forgotten. Margarete's letters to him changed in tone from the bantering of a honeymooner ("You naughty soldier of fortune, you must come to this part of the world sometimes") to the pleading of a worried wife ("Something's always going wrong. I save so hard, but the money's like everything

Polemist Alfred Rosenberg harangues a crowd around 1920. He influenced Himmler by elevating the theory of Nordic supremacy to a religion, whose devotees considered it their mission to assail Jews and other supposedly alien groups.

else") to abject despair ("O my dear, what is going to become of me?").

While Himmler labored over details of uniform and pedigree, the membership of his new order increased only slowly. The leaders of the Nazi party were locked in struggles for power in far-off Berlin, and economic trouble was again besetting Germany. The reckless borrowing and heated expansion of the 1920s gave way to a deepening worldwide depression and the agonies of massive unemployment. More than a million Germans were out of work in 1929; their number would rise to three million a year later and would peak at six million in 1933. Such distress provided fertile ground for the Nazis' politics of fear.

But as fear mounted, the Nazis found they were not immune to it. By 1930 membership in the SA ranged between 60,000 and 100,000 Storm Troopers who wanted both more money, which the financially strapped party did not have, and more power, which Hitler would yield to no one. In one intraparty dispute, the Brownshirts actually attacked Nazi headquarters in Berlin, and to Hitler's intense embarrassment, civil police had to be called to restore order. Furious, he took personal command of the SA and in January of 1931 recalled its former commander—none other than Ernst Röhm—to serve as chief of staff.

Himmler was no more interested in Röhm's return than he had been in his old friend's departure, but he must have been delighted by what Hitler did next. The Führer made the loyal SS independent of the unruly SA. "No SA commander is entitled to give orders to the SS," he decreed, stipulating that the role of the SS was "primarily to carry out police duties within the party." It was hardly the grandiose view of a quasi-religious order that Himmler had been cultivating, although it did confer on the SS a special status. For the moment, however, all Himmler did to grasp the advantage was to introduce a snappy new uniform—mostly black instead of SA brown—to emphasize the SS independence. Not until the next year did the products of Himmler's long ruminations begin to emerge—first in the form of the Engagement and Marriage Order of the SS, announced on December 31, 1931. Under this regulation, no member of the SS could marry until his genealogy had been analyzed by a new SS department, directed by Darré and eventually designated the Office of Race and Settlement. This would ensure that the individual met the high genetic standards of the SS and the master race to come.

Then the prospective bride would be investigated. She and her family would have to prove that they were of pure Aryan blood, uncontaminated at least since 1750 by the presence of any Jewish, Slavic, or similarly inferior

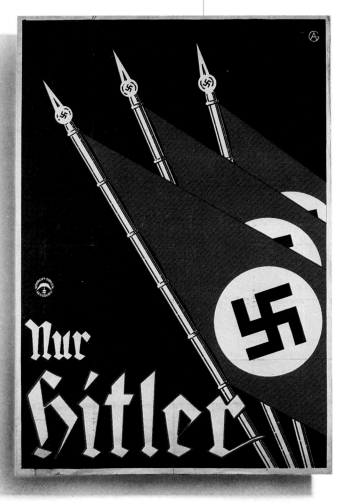

ancestors. The woman would further have to demonstrate that she was free of all mental and physical disease, and submit to an exhaustive examination, including fertility testing, by SS doctors. Only after a couple had successfully completed all these tests could an SS marriage take place. It occurred to Himmler, apparently, that some skeptics might not take his racial theories seriously. "It is clear to the SS that with this command it has taken a step of great significance," he proclaimed in publishing the marriage order. "Derision, scorn, and failure to understand do not move us; the future belongs to us!"

To be sure, the outlandish policy drew ridicule—from Hitler, among others. But Himmler's claim on the future was soon affirmed; the SS enjoyed an infusion of recruits, especially from the middle class, who were again caught in a downward-spiraling economy. Membership in Himmler's curious combination of fraternity, regiment, and utopian community soared from 10,000 at the end of 1931 to more than 40,000 six months later. Yet the quiet growth of the SS remained overshadowed by the noisy expansion of both the Nazi party, which was becoming a major force in German politics, and the SA, whose ranks continued to swell with men who were out of work. While Himmler laid plans and arranged orga-

nizational tables in Munich, tumultuous events ran their course in Berlin.

In successive elections called by the tottering government, Hitler ran for the presidency and failed, then maneuvered for a legislative majority and the chancellorship, failing again. In his eagerness, he unleashed the SA, now 400,000 members strong, and precipitated the worst violence Germany had yet seen. The Storm Troopers ran riot, battling the communists, socialists, and other factions in the streets. During June and July of 1932, nearly 500 pitched battles took place in Prussia alone, with 82 people killed and some 400 wounded. The Nazis emerged as the largest party in the Reichstag after the July national elections, but were still far short of a majority. Hitler refused to join a coalition government, and when he forced

SS men go shirtless in mock compliance with an April 1932 decree by Chancellor Heinrich Brüning outlawing Hitler's uniformed contingents. The order was rescinded the following month, after Nazi intrigue helped replace Brüning.

still another election in November, the party lost two million votes and thirty-four seats. Gregor Strasser, arguing that Hitler's intransigence had crippled the party's chances, quit in disgust. Hitler simply assumed his popular deputy's offices and threw out all those who remained loyal to Strasser, thus further diminishing the National Socialist party. The Führer seemed to be bent on political self-destruction.

But President Paul von Hindenburg, desperate to end the country's agony, reluctantly appointed Hitler chancellor on January 30, 1933. Given a tenuous hold on power—shared with the conservatives, limited by law, overseen by the president—Hitler moved with blinding speed to secure his grip. Determined to gain control of the legislature at any price, he called a new election and once again unleashed the Brownshirts to hound his opponents—especially the increasingly popular communists, whom he blamed for a February 27 fire that gutted the Reichstag building in Berlin. The day after the fire, Hitler persuaded the aging Hindenburg to sign a decree, "for the protection of the people and the state," that abolished guarantees of individual liberty and authorized the central government to assume complete power in the federal states if necessary. Now instead of merely having his foes beaten, Hitler had them arrested.

Still the National Socialists did not win a majority of seats in the Reichstag. But the Nazis did elect enough deputies, and intimidated enough of the others, to form a temporary coalition. And before anyone could draw

breath, Hitler rammed through the pliant new Reichstag an emergency act transferring all budgetary and legislative powers to his cabinet for a period of four years. The bill was passed on March 23, 1933, and with that, democracy in Germany expired.

In Berlin, Nazis thundered through the corridors of power, clamoring for the favor of their Führer, seizing positions in the government, savaging one another's reputations, and making endless deals to accumulate impressive personal titles. In Munich, where Himmler sat, everything was quiet. The SS had served Hitler faithfully and well. Twice they had fought pitched battles with rebellious members of the SA. In 1931 a grateful Hitler had written to Daluege, the Berlin SS commander, the sentence that became the organization's motto: "SS man, thy loyalty is thine honor." And an exultant Himmler had proclaimed to his subordinates, "Our Führer knows the value of the SS. We are his favorite and most valuable organization because we have never let him down."

But in 1933, when the time came for dividing spoils, Himmler and his Schutzstaffel were virtually ignored. Himmler was made acting president of the Munich police and, later, head of the Bavarian political police. But those who had stood closest to the center of power rose the fastest. Hermann Göring, the World War I flying ace who had been an intimate of Hitler since the days of the Beer Hall Putsch, became a minister of the national government, the most powerful minister of the Prussian state government, and if that were not enough, declared himself chief forester of the Third Reich. Goebbels became minister of propaganda and created for himself a new ministry of culture.

Himmler, with typical single-mindedness, immersed himself in police work and found it entirely to his liking. He recalled that his grandfather had been a member of the royal police in Munich and soon discovered that law enforcement provided opportunities for self-aggrandizement. With the help of a dedicated young assistant named Reinhard Heydrich, he started to maneuver for the control of police departments in other German states. He began to think about a single, national police force under his control. Himmler realized that to succeed, he would first have to elbow his way into the circle of power around the Führer. He owed the existence of his organization to Hitler's personal fears, and it did not require deep thinking to conclude that his best course would be to stimulate those apprehensions again. At once, Himmler began to discover and report to Berlin various plots against the Führer. Adolf Hitler had always been fearful for his own life, and Himmler's rapid-fire warnings—of a planned coup, an intended hand-grenade attack, then "information from Switzerland" of

various communist threats—made Hitler eager for more protection, which Himmler was glad to provide.

To augment Hitler's personal guard, a select contingent of 120 men was sent to Berlin under the command of a Bavarian SS officer, Josef "Sepp" Dietrich. Henceforth, any visitor to the Führer had to pass the hard gaze of at least three members of this *Leibstandarte,* or bodyguard. The SS had moved closer to the inner circle. The next step was easy. If Hitler needed and deserved the protection of the elite SS, then so too did other important government officials. Before long, Himmler had placed special detachments of guards all over Germany. Now his extended period of planning and organizing finally began to pay dividends. Whereas the SA had been uncontrollable, the black-shirted men of the SS were superbly disciplined and utterly loyal to Hitler.

The comparison was soon drawn even more starkly as Röhm's SA grasped for power over the army. Röhm had always seen himself as eventual commander of the country's armed forces, the wielder of such power that political titles, by comparison, would be mere window dressing. Hitler tried to pacify his longtime comrade by ordering the army and the SA to work out a compromise by which the status of the SA would be raised to that of militia. But the effort failed, and the Reichswehr remained the only force in Germany authorized to bear arms, a privilege it jealously guarded. Early in 1934, Röhm insisted again on merging the SA with the army. Hitler pleaded for peace between the two, and in a stormy meeting of the principals, Röhm agreed. But as soon as Hitler left the room, Röhm delivered a treasonous tirade: "What that ridiculous corporal says means nothing to us. I have not the slightest intention of keeping this agreement. Hitler is a traitor, and at the very least must go on leave."

Hitler, meanwhile, laid plans to eviscerate the troublesome SA. He had ambitions that went far beyond the borders of Germany and believed that only the established officer corps had the training, ability, and discipline

Nazi followers throng the stadium at Nuremberg on Party Day in September 1933 to hail their Führer, now chancellor of Germany. Most of those assembled are members of the SA, but SS men with their distinctive black caps can be seen at right, guarding the way with arms linked.

to rearm Germany and carry out his international vision. Moreover, on the death of the mortally ill president Hindenburg, Hitler intended to grab the powers of the presidency, a move that only the military had the power to prevent. And in exchange for the support of the army, the Führer was more than ready to sacrifice the SA.

But Röhm and his Brownshirts remained an obtrusive, threatening presence everywhere in Germany. As shows of strength, Röhm encouraged lengthy parades and massive rallies of his unruly, brown-shirted legions. Meanwhile, luxuriating in his power, he made no attempt to mitigate or conceal his sometimes raucous homosexual liaisons. His posture was regarded as so menacing that the Nazi leadership turned increasingly for protection to Himmler and the SS.

One surprising new ally of Himmler in these circumstances was Hermann Göring. The two men had been on a collision course, with Göring plotting to organize a national police force from his home base in Prussia, just as Himmler had been planning to do from Bavaria. Göring's new political police organization—the Geheime Staatspolizei, or Gestapo for short—was already well known. But Göring realized that he could not deal with the Storm Troopers on his own, and as part of a 1934 nationalization of state governments, he agreed to make Himmler deputy chief of the Gestapo. By the end of April, Himmler had become, in effect, boss of the political police in all of Germany.

Now firmly inside the Führer's circle, Himmler moved his residence to Berlin (while sending his deserted family to live in a house on a lake near Munich). He and Göring settled in at the elbows of Hitler and turned baleful eyes on Röhm and the SA. Himmler toured the outposts of his SS network, lecturing his subordinates on the need for complete loyalty. Meanwhile, his second in command, Heydrich, combed the files for incriminating evidence against Röhm and the other leaders of the SA. The SS commander at a new concentration camp at Dachau, Theodor Eicke, prepared his men

to fight the SA in Munich and its environs. Eicke was also ordered to prepare lists of "unwanted people" to be shot. Himmler and Göring compiled their own lists of so-called enemies of the state. There ensued lengthy, enthusiastic debates over the fate of scores of individuals—barely half of them members of the SA—and an avid exchanging of lists among men who had been friends and beneficiaries of the condemned.

Hitler's role in these clandestine preparations bore no resemblance to the picture he liked to present of steely decision making and efficient execution. On the contrary, he could not decide what to do about the SA, when to do it, or whether to do anything at all. Röhm was one of Hitler's oldest and closest associates—the only one with whom he used the familiar form of address *du*—and for a time he could not bring himself to break with the man, let alone have him shot as part of a purge of SA leaders.

Hitler's subordinates were not troubled by such compunctions. Himmler had known and admired Röhm for years, but now Röhm stood between him and more power for his beloved SS; Röhm had to die. Göring was determined to become commander of the armed forces and had no qualms about using murder to clear the field of competitors. Heydrich was interested in only two things: who was in power and what dirty work he wanted done. Heydrich's first-born child had two godfathers—Röhm and Himmler. Now one of them had to go.

The plans and the roster of cities across Germany where SS teams would strike were quickly prepared. Sepp Dietrich and two handpicked companies of men were ordered to report to southern Bavaria, where Röhm and some of his principal lieutenants were relaxing at a spa. Dietrich visited army headquarters to request weapons and transportation for a "most important mission ordered by the Führer." The army complied, and Dietrich and his men planned to link up with Eicke's command from the Dachau concentration camp.

Himmler and Heydrich, with Göring's able assistance, stepped up their campaign to justify what the SS was about to do by producing a flow of spurious evidence of a plot to overthrow Hitler. The evidence was carefully fed to Hitler and the army commanders in order to stiffen their resolve to deal with Röhm. If Hitler needed any further motivation to go through with the purge, he received it on June 21, when President Hindenburg, appalled by the continued outrageous behavior of Röhm and the Brownshirts, vowed that unless order was restored he would declare martial law and turn power over to the army.

On June 28, with the time for action critically near, Hitler and Göring went to a wedding in western Germany. Himmler began to telephone constantly from Berlin with ever more frightening allegations of an immi-

Smiles from SA chief Röhm *(third from left)* and Reichsführer-SS Himmler *(to Röhm's left)* mask their rivalry in 1933. The diminutive man beside Himmler is Josef "Sepp" Dietrich, commander of Hitler's bodyguard and a key participant in the coming purge.

nent coup. Whether this was an elaborate charade conducted with Hitler's cooperation and intended for public consumption later, or part of the campaign by Himmler and Göring to keep the Führer on track, is not clear. But at length, early on June 29, Hitler announced, "I've had enough. I shall make an example of them."

With that, Göring returned to Berlin, and Hitler, having first ordered Dietrich's men to move, flew to Munich and drove to the resort where Röhm was staying. Arriving just after dawn, Hitler stormed into Röhm's room with an escort of police detectives. Brandishing a pistol, Hitler accused his old comrade of treason. While the dazed Röhm dressed, Hitler rousted out another high SA official and his male companion. After raging at them for a time, Hitler had the astonished officers packed off to prison.

Meanwhile, all over Germany death squads and round-up details went calling. Their movements were superbly orchestrated by Himmler, who, with the assistance of Heydrich, was showing for the first time what he was really capable of accomplishing. Sepp Dietrich went to the Stadelheim

Prison in Munich with a detail of men—he had selected "six good shots," he recalled, "to ensure that nothing messy happened"—and hauled out six of the top SA officers. One of them called, "Sepp, my friend, what on earth's happening? We are completely innocent." The reply was a click of the heels and a coldly worded "You have been condemned to death by the Führer. Heil Hitler!" The shooting began.

It was a time not only for dealing with the SA, but for settling old scores with a long list of other enemies. SS men found one of the Bavarian government leaders who had foiled the Beer Hall Putsch in 1923, hauled him onto a heath, and killed him with a pickax. Strasser, who Himmler feared might still become reconciled with Hitler, was seized in Berlin and thrown into a cell, where he was shot from behind; his death was proclaimed a suicide. One death squad went out searching for a Munich physician who had supported Otto Strasser; by tragic mistake they seized a man with a similar name who was a doctor of philosophy and a music critic. The man's body was returned to his home later—in a coffin that his family was ordered never to open.

The purge that came to be known as the Night of the Long Knives lasted a little more than two days. During that time, without any semblance of legal proceedings, nearly 200 people were seized and quickly killed; some estimates of the number murdered are much higher. From the army, from the office of the president of the German republic, from the courts and the police agencies and the surviving officers of the SA, there came only scattered protests. "In this hour," Hitler could boast later, "I was responsible for the fate of the German people, and thereby I became the supreme judge of the German people."

Yet at a very late hour—midmorning on July 1—the supreme judge had not yet been able to decide the fate of Ernst Röhm. The previous day, Hitler had summoned a meeting of unpurged SA leaders in Munich and raved (literally foaming at the mouth, an awed member of the audience reported) that he had ordered Röhm's execution. But in fact Hitler had been unable to do it, and before leaving Munich he gave his word to Röhm's former commanding officer that the life of the SA chief would be spared. Back in Berlin, however, Himmler and Göring tried to convince their Führer that he could not afford to let Röhm live. They feared that Röhm might be convincing when he claimed that there never had been an SA plot to overthrow the Hitler government. At last, Hitler overcame his squeamishness and gave the order.

The job was assigned to Theodor Eicke. Flanked by two henchmen, he strode into the cell at Stadelheim Prison where Röhm sat

A banner headline on June 30, 1934, proclaims that Röhm has been "arrested and deposed." The paper names Viktor Lutze as Röhm's successor but, by listing seven SA renegades (*bottom*) who have just been shot, emphasizes that Lutze and his Storm Troopers must show Hitler "blind obedience."

on an iron bed, barechested and sweating. "You have forfeited your life!" Eicke intoned. "The Führer gives you one more chance to draw the conclusions." Then, as Hitler had specifically instructed, Eicke laid in front of Röhm some newspapers containing accounts of the Night of the Long Knives—and a loaded pistol.

The SS men waited in the hallway outside the cell for fifteen silent minutes. Then Eicke opened the door and shouted, "Chief of staff, get ready!" The SS men shot twice, at point-blank range. Röhm fell, groaning, "My Führer, my Führer." Eicke was contemptuous. "You should have thought of that earlier. It's too late now." He stomped away, secure in the knowledge that he had served Himmler and Hitler well by killing their closest political associate.

Two days later, Hitler's cabinet passed a one-sentence law: "The measures taken on June 30, July 1 and 2 to suppress treasonable activities are legally considered to have been taken in emergency defense of the state." Thus the Blood Purge received a veneer of legality. On July 20 Hitler granted Himmler and his men their reward. "In view of the great services rendered by the SS, particularly in connection with the events of June 30, 1934," he decreed, "I hereby promote the SS to the status of independent organization." Back at their desks, Heinrich Himmler and Reinhard Heydrich consulted their file cards and turned their attention to the remaining enemies of the Third Reich. ✚

Dark Rites
of the
Mystic Order

To Heinrich Himmler, the SS was more than a clique of party zealots committed to crushing the foes of the Third Reich; it was an exalted "order of Nordic men"— a mystic brotherhood inspired by tales of Teutonic knig[...] medieval legends. To foster fraternal devotion within the SS, Himmler staged splendid initiation rites. Each year, men bound for military-SS units took their oath in Hitler's presence at 10 p.m. on November [...], the anniversary of the 1923 Munich putsch. Beneath pillars of flame that lent a lurid sacramental light to the proceedings (right), the recruits pledged "obedience unto death." One observer recalled the moment [...] ears came to my eyes when, by the light of the torches, thousands of voices repeated the oath in chorus. It was like a prayer."

For all its power, this ceremony alone could not ensure lasting loyalty. Himmler noted, "A sworn oath is not of itself enough. It is essential that every man be committed to the very roots of his being." To that end, Himmler instituted rites meant to bind an initiate ever more securely to the order. Worthy SS veterans received rings and weapons inscribed with symbols culled from German legend. SS men were married, and their infants named, in ceremonies designed to supplant Christian sacraments—an approach Himmler also applied to church holidays, replacing them with pagan festivals. Himmler's ultimate reach into the past was a renovated castle, inspired by King Arthur's Camelot, with a hall dedicated to the order's twelve leading knights. Less exalted members were assured that after death they, too, would be honored by their brothers.

Not all of Himmler's occult rites were embraced wholeheartedly by the SS men, many of whom remained professed Christians. Yet most initiates learned to play their parts and abide even those customs they found peculiar—a useful exercise for men who were expected to meet death obediently and inflict it without question.

Helmeted SS recruits in 1938 prepare to take their oath as a

group at Munich's Feldherrnhalle, its stage lit by torches symbolizing the martyrs of the putsch fifteen years earlier.

Most recruits who took the SS oath, at either a mass gathering or a more modest ceremony *(right)*, assumed the common rank of SS man. The only distinction they could claim was the right to wear the black uniform, a smart outfit that lured many initiates. Those who served faithfully or rose to positions of command became eligible for more exclusive tokens *(below)* featuring insignia that evoked Germany's heroic heritage. Their daggers carried the inscription "My honor is loyalty," a motto suggested by Hitler that echoed the knightly vows of Teutonic legend. And SS men wore rings and swords decorated with mystic runes—symbols employed by the warlike peoples of northern Europe in pagan times.

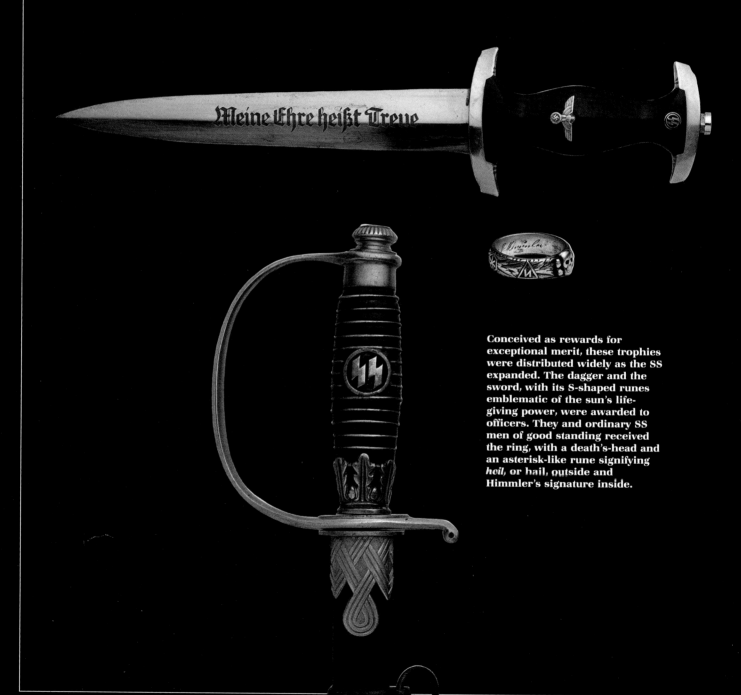

Conceived as rewards for exceptional merit, these trophies were distributed widely as the SS expanded. The dagger and the sword, with its S-shaped runes emblematic of the sun's life-giving power, were awarded to officers. They and ordinary SS men of good standing received the ring, with a death's-head and an asterisk-like rune signifying *heil*, or hail, outside and Himmler's signature inside.

Touching a consecrated flag, recruits for the *allgemeine*, or nonmilitary, SS swear obedience in a ceremony in Hamburg.

Himmler tenders sword and scabbard to newly commissioned SS officers in 1937. The swords were worn only at ceremonies.

Secular Services for Select Couples

Himmler's mania for racial purity, coupled with his contempt for Christian sacraments—which he considered fit only for the meek— yielded an exotic program to foster proper SS families. Before marrying, an SS man had to prove that his fiancée shared his Aryan heritage. Church weddings were replaced by pagan SS rites presided over by the bridegroom's commander. Similar protocol governed the "christening" of infants, some of whom were born in Lebensborn centers, free SS maternity homes set up to encourage conception.

More than a few members found the marriage regulations impossible to live with. In 1937 alone, 300 men were expelled from the SS for marrying without approval.

An SS corporal and his bride pass through a somber arcade of saluting brethren.

To boost the birthrate, both the SS and the Nazi party ran spacious maternity homes and nurseries such as this sunlit crèche.

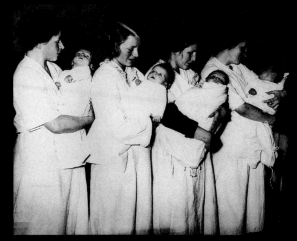

Women cradle their infants at a home in Mecklenburg. A number of those who lay in at these centers were unwed mothers.

In a name-giving rite at an altar adorned with a portrait of Hitler, an SS officer places his hand on a newborn.

In a 1936 memorandum, Himmler set forth a list of approved holidays based on pagan and political precedents and meant to wean SS members from their reliance on Christian festivities. The list included April 20, Hitler's birthday; May Day and the summer solstice; a harvest feast; and November 9, the anniversary of the Beer Hall Putsch.

Climaxing the year in Himmler's scheme was the winter solstice, or Yuletide, an event that brought SS folk together at candlelit banquet tables and around raging bonfires that harked back to German tribal rites. Yet these Christmastime blazes held no promise of peace. As the SS newspaper, *The Black Corps*, noted in 1938, "The Magi of the East today cast frightened glances in the direction of the bright flames that we are lighting in the nights of the winter solstice."

SS guards and office workers at Neuengamme concentration camp, near Berlin, gather for a Yuletide feast in 1943. At each

Silhouetted against a Yuletide bonfire in 1937, Himmler *(left)* stands beside two officers holding a festal wreath.

setting is wine, a loaf of bread, and a Yule candleholder, produced by the inmates of another camp, Dachau.

In 1934 Himmler selected a moldering clifftop castle in Westphalia to serve as the SS high temple. Known as Wewelsburg, the seventeenth-century fortress was overhauled at a cost of more than three million dollars, a sizable sum considering that labor was extracted free from concentration-camp inmates. The sanctum included a 12,000-volume library of Aryan lore and a cavernous dining hall with an Arthurian round table for Himmler and twelve trusted lieutenants. Reportedly, each knight of Himmler's round table received a coat of arms; at the man's death, his emblem was to be incinerated in the pit of the Supreme Leaders' Hall *(below)*, and the ashes placed in an urn atop one of twelve pedestals there.

Windows at Wewelsburg allow a mystic light into the memorial hall, capped with a swastika.

Wewelsburg, shown here before its restoration, served as both a retreat for Himmler and a center for racial research.

Members of an SS honor guard, wearing the SA-style brown shirts that some in Himmler's corps wore as late as 1934, flank

The SS Way of Death

In death as in life, the SS sought to distinguish its members from the uninitiated. For SS men who had renounced church ties—as a majority of those in the armed units did—an alternative to Christian burial was devised. After a silent vigil *(left)*, the deceased was conveyed to the cemetery in a horse-drawn carriage, eulogized by his commander, and interred as comrades sang the SS hymn.

Once the war began, such pomp became impractical. But rune-shaped SS grave markers *(below)* continued to identify the fallen as men of a special order.

An Iron Cross marks the grave of an SS man who died in Russia on November 2, 1942. The marker combines the Y-shaped runic symbol for life and its inverted form, the gable-shaped sign of death.

the swastika-draped coffin of their comrade during a candlelight vigil.

TWO

Forging the Ultimate Police Force

ever had police inspector Franz Josef Huber felt such anxiety. In March of 1933 neither Huber nor many other Germans yet knew what to make of their new chancellor, Adolf Hitler, but Huber had more reason than most for apprehension. A member of the political department of the Munich police, he had spent years doing everything possible to stymie the Nazi party and its offshoots, the SA and the SS, going so far as to make derogatory remarks in public about Hitler himself. He was well acquainted with the methods of Heinrich Himmler, who had just been appointed police commissioner of Munich, and of Himmler's icy-visaged assistant, Reinhard Heydrich. Thus he was not surprised, he said later, when one of the Nazis' first acts after taking power was to send him "the so-called blue letter—suspension from duty pending decision on my further employment."

If losing his job was the worst that befell him, Huber would be thankful. But now he had been ordered to report to his department's new boss, Heydrich. The summons filled Huber with dread; he knew that throughout Bavaria and all of Germany, opponents of the Nazis were being rounded up by the hundreds, many to be tortured or shot. After the interview with Heydrich, he might be among them.

Heart pounding, Huber sat opposite the blond twenty-nine-year-old who had suddenly assumed power over hundreds of thousands of Bavarians. Heydrich "was a tall, impressive figure," recalled a subordinate, "with a broad, unusually high forehead, small restless eyes as crafty as an animal's and of uncanny power, a long predatory nose, a wide, full-lipped mouth. His hands were slender and rather too long—they made one think of the legs of a spider. His splendid figure was marred by the breadth of his hips, a disturbingly feminine effect that made him appear even more sinister."

Heydrich let Huber wait in silence for a long agonizing minute. Huber could see that Heydrich was perusing a list of names; some were marked with a small cross, the significance of which Huber could only guess. At last, gazing at Huber as if at some insect he might squash, Heydrich asked, "Which Huber are you?" Trying to steady his voice, Huber repeated his full

A muzzled German shepherd joins an SS man *(right)* and a Berlin police officer on patrol in March of 1933. In the months to come, the SS would unleash its new police powers against thousands of citizens, confining them without trial as "enemies of the state."

name. Heydrich consulted his list again, locked Huber in his chilling gaze, and pronounced judgment: The inspector was to return to his duties.

Thus the astonished Huber was launched on a second career, during which he would become a high-ranking policeman in a police state and would transfer his zeal from harassing the Nazis to hounding their enemies. As Heydrich had perceived, Huber was a thoroughgoing professional, and Heydrich needed such men if he were to fulfill his own mission in the nazification of Germany. Just as Himmler had conceived of an elite corps within the Nazi party—the SS—and had labored for years to prepare it for ultimate power, so Heydrich had nurtured the vision of a select group within the SS, a police force that would protect the SS from enemies within and without. In the dream's full form, this unit's job would be to purify the German people, purging the nation not only of active enemies of the Nazis but of critics, dissenters, and even those who fit a category called "work-shy."

But while Himmler remained obsessed with racial purity and the breeding of a master race, Heydrich took a more pragmatic approach to accumulating power. He wanted a force of hard men who would be rigorous in ferreting out enemies, whether criminal or political; unquestioning in following orders and accepting new definitions of who constituted the enemy; ruthlessly analytical in pursuing suspicious leads; and brutal in stamping out opposition. Heydrich sought his men among the likes of Huber; with their help and by dint of his own twisted idealism and unceasing work, he would forge one of history's most powerful and dreaded police forces—the Gestapo.

Before anything else, Reinhard Tristan Eugen Heydrich was a musician. He was surrounded by music from the time of his birth in 1904. (Almost four years Himmler's junior, he was too young to take any part in World War I.) His mother was an accomplished pianist, his father an opera singer, a composer, and an ardent admirer of Richard Wagner. Together, the parents ran a music conservatory in the eastern city of Halle. Reinhard became a first-class violinist; years later, he would remain capable of picking up an instrument and bowing a melancholy air with technical skill and great feeling, sometimes weeping copiously as he played.

Reinhard Heydrich secretly used his position as security chief of the SS to keep tabs on Nazi leaders as well as their foes. He even maintained files on Himmler and Adolf Hitler.

His schoolboy years were not happy. Raised a devout Catholic in a heavily Protestant city, he found himself in that most dreaded of schoolyard situations—a member of a minority. (For good measure, his tormentors soon assigned him to another minority, taunting him as a Jew—a charge derived from the fact that his widowed grandmother had, late in life, married a man with what was regarded as a Jewish-sounding name.) Heydrich was further burdened with a falsetto voice; his peers poked fun at him, and the bigger boys occasionally beat him up. His excellence in academics gained him few admirers. Nor could he take much comfort from his family's elevated social status and elegant residence; his mother was a disciplinarian who believed in the educational and religious benefits of frequent thrashings. Reinhard became a sullen, introverted youth.

He came to appreciate his family's financial comfort only after it was obliterated by the inflation that followed war and revolution. As a fifteen-year-old in 1919 he joined Halle's Civil Defense Corps, which was organized to fight local communists, but he saw no action. This brief encounter with military life, as well as summer vacations on the shore of the Baltic Sea, intensified his desire to become a naval officer. Small but elite, the postwar German navy had much to offer: free education to a son in a financially strapped family, prestige to a persecuted youth, and a guaranteed pension after ten years of service. In March 1922 he became a naval cadet.

At Kiel, Germany's chief naval base, Heydrich was plunged back into the miseries of the schoolyard. He was taller than six feet now, but awkward and bony, and his high-pitched voice, abstemious habits, and passion for music drew a steady barrage of ridicule that frequently referred to his presumed Jewish background. The other cadets called him "Moses Handel" or, in mockery of his bleating voice, "billy goat." One instructor, who liked to make his cadets fall facefirst during training as a test of courage, frequently summoned Heydrich late at night to play his violin, always demanding the same sentimental Toselli serenata. Heydrich never forgot the despotic instructor, whom he described as one of the "little, fat, round-headed racial types of the East," or the tune; he automatically switched off the radio any time it came on the air.

Grimly, haughtily, Heydrich persevered. Even more than Himmler, he punished himself into a proficiency beyond his natural gifts. In 1923 his training continued on the cruiser *Berlin.* Heydrich was invited by Wilhelm Canaris, the ship's first officer, to participate in his wife's musical evenings and was thus brought into contact with local society. Heydrich's musical talent, quick mind, good looks—his ungainly skinniness having matured into a comely leanness—provided him with an engrossing new hobby: seducing women. There were risks in this for a cadet; a shipmate recalled

that on shore leave in Barcelona a young lady of good family not only rebuffed Heydrich's advances but slapped him and complained to his commanding officer, who ordered Heydrich to make an official apology.

For a time, neither Heydrich's limitations nor his gaffes seriously impaired his progress. In 1926 he was commissioned a second lieutenant and assigned as a signals officer on the obsolete battleship *Schleswig-Holstein*, flagship of Germany's Baltic Fleet. Although his confidence grew and he was able to unbend slightly, he was still teased by fellow officers about his thin voice, his subordinates complained about his arrogance, and he remained a driven man. "He was never content with what he had achieved," a friend recalled of Heydrich's navy years. "His impulse was always for more. As a lieutenant he was already dreaming of becoming an admiral."

Similarly, there could never be enough women in Heydrich's life, and in 1930 his penchant for womanizing led to disaster. At a rowing-club ball, he met a woman named Lina von Osten. A romance ensued, and in December the two announced their engagement. The news caused distress to another young woman who believed she was engaged to marry Heydrich. When he coldly rejected her protests, her father, a naval shipyard superintendent with influence at the admiralty in Berlin, lodged a complaint. Heydrich found himself under investigation; no German naval officer would be permitted to treat a German woman in such dishonorable fashion.

Heydrich told a court of honor that he was innocent and that the woman was lying. He responded to questions with such undisguised contempt, however, that he was reprimanded for insubordination. His attitude prompted the court to conclude that although his offense was relatively minor, it called into question "the possibility of such an officer remaining in the navy." There was no doubt in the mind of the navy's commanding admiral, Erich Raeder; upon receiving the court's findings in April of 1931, he sentenced First Lieutenant Heydrich to "dismissal for impropriety."

Heydrich was crushed. Not only was the blow unexpected, but it came just a year before he would have been eligible for a pension. He could not bring himself to accept one of the few civilian jobs—such as sailing instructor at a yacht club—that were available to him in a country teeming with the unemployed. He remained engaged to the woman for whom he had dashed his career, and she remained loyal despite her parents' opposition to her marrying the disgraced young man. "Discharge from the navy was the heaviest blow of his life," Lina recalled years later. "It was not the lost earning power that weighed on him, but the fact that with every fiber of his being he had clung to his career as an officer."

Heydrich's mother, who appeared to be concerned most about her son's loss of social standing (and who thought Lina an inferior marriage pros-

Heydrich offers a toy ball to his infant son as his wife Lina watches at their Munich home in 1934. On the job, Heydrich relied more on threats than inducements, prompting even callous SS men to refer to him as the "blond beast."

pect), cast about for suitable opportunities. A family friend proved to have high-level contacts in the Nazi party and its SS, whose members were increasingly regarded as a social, as well as political, elite. This direction was approved by Lina; she and her brother had been enthusiastic Nazis for some time. Heydrich agreed to join the party and accepted an interview arranged with the new Reichsführer, or national commander, of the SS.

Himmler at this time was looking for the right person to set up an intelligence service for his new order, now about 10,000 strong. The elections of 1930 had made the National Socialists the second-largest party in the politically splintered country, and their activities were under intense scrutiny by the government, other competing parties, and the press. Himmler already had a prospect for the internal-security job—a man who was in fact an infiltrator working for the political department of the Munich police (undoubtedly with the knowledge of then Inspector Huber). Apparently, Himmler regretted agreeing to interview Heydrich; on the day before the appointment, he canceled it. But Heydrich, braced by his fiancée, showed up anyway, and Himmler reluctantly saw him.

Himmler, who had no practical experience in the area, mistakenly believed the young applicant had served in naval intelligence—although Heydrich's actual exposure to the subject was limited to a classroom course. Impressed by the man's Nordic looks and cool self-confidence, Himmler decided on a schoolmaster-like test: He asked Heydrich how he envisioned an SS security service and gave him twenty minutes to draw up a plan for one. Heydrich patched together what he remembered from the navy and the spy adventures he had read, couched it in military terminology, and presented it to Himmler. Whether the SS commander was pleased more by Heydrich's physical traits or the results of the twenty-minute exercise remains unclear, but Heydrich was hired. (The informant who did not get the job committed suicide after the Nazis came to power.)

Heydrich moved into Nazi party headquarters in Munich, called Brown House. His salary was meager—far less, for example, than that of a sailing

instructor—and his office facilities consisted of a chair and a kitchen table in a shared room with only one typewriter. But he soon showed a remarkable aptitude for his new line of work. Calmly, methodically, Heydrich began to build on Himmler's loose file of enemy operatives and to devise plans for dealing with them. In many ways, he seemed a distilled version of his boss; whereas Heydrich was a fanatical worker, Himmler was merely compulsive, and compared with his shy but more accessible employer, Heydrich seemed to be a dedicated recluse. Moreover, Heydrich had the ability to evince deadly menace while Himmler, try as he might, was incapable of appearing much more than petulant.

More important, however, was Heydrich's quick grasp of the maze of political alliances in which he was operating and the motivations and loyalties of the people he was watching. According to Himmler's masseur and confidant Felix Kersten, Heydrich's mind was "a living card index, a brain that held all the threads and wove them together." After only a few weeks of organizing and augmenting a haphazard collection of reports, accusations, rumors, suspicions, and denunciations, Heydrich electrified a meeting of SS leaders in August of 1931 by declaring that the Nazi party was riddled with spies and saboteurs. It must be purged, he said. Every SS unit must have a security detachment to weed out the disloyal.

There was an important later stipulation. Rival intelligence and counterespionage agencies were striving for supremacy within the Nazi party, and they all were using party regulars as agents. Heydrich wanted to recruit his own people. To demonstrate why this was necessary, he uncovered an infiltrator, another Munich police officer, who as a party member had access to Brown House. Heydrich converted the man to a double agent.

Himmler, thoroughly impressed, gave Heydrich some staff help (although not a typewriter of his own) and allowed him to move to a separate office, where he added constantly to a growing collection of boxes filled with index cards. There were not only more cards, but more categories of possible enmity or rot: aristocrats, Catholics, communists, conservatives, politically active Jews, Freemasons, and Nazis afflicted with poor motivation, large debts, or latent scandals. And the interconnections needed watching. Jewish communists, for example, or socialists who were also Freemasons went into a special "poison" file. The work was only briefly interrupted by his wedding to Lina von Osten in December of 1931 (just days before the announcement of the new SS marriage order).

Heydrich won rapid promotion; by December he had become an SS major. But in June of 1932 his new career suffered a jarring, potentially fatal setback. Once again someone was calling Heydrich a Jew: A Nazi official in Halle had picked up the old rumors. Consternation swept SS headquarters

at the thought of the head of security being an agent of world Jewry, and a full-scale genealogical investigation ensued. Its curt conclusion: "Heydrich is of German origin and free from any colored or Jewish blood."

By July Heydrich not only had organized his counterspies into an organization called the Sicherheitsdienst (SD), or Security Service, but had eased them out of the SS chain of command, making them responsible only to him. He, of course, reported to Himmler, who rewarded him with promotion to SS colonel. The two men had a touchy relationship. Heydrich knew that his advancement depended on the goodwill of his Nazi employer, and he no doubt remembered that insolence toward his superiors had got him cashiered from the navy. He treated Himmler with excessive deference, while raging in private that his boss was a dolt, "always maneuvering and trimming his sails; he won't take responsibility." His private antidote for the galling necessity of submission, Heydrich told his wife, was to imagine Himmler "in his underpants; then everything's all right."

Himmler, meanwhile, felt besieged by his assistant. Heydrich prepared recommendations with exhaustive research, then presented them with a bombardment of facts and carefully constructed arguments. "Sometimes I had the impression," reported a contemporary, "that after one of these expositions Himmler was quite overwhelmed." Unable to rebut his assistant, the SS chief almost always gave in, even when he disagreed utterly and had no intention of carrying out the proposal. He would simply change the orders later, claiming he had received new instructions from Hitler. Himmler did lose his temper on occasion. "You and your logic," he once exploded at Heydrich. "We never hear about anything but your logic. Everything I propose, you batter down with your logic. I am fed up with you and your cold, rational criticism." Heydrich, appalled, backed down. Himmler soon forgot his outburst; it is unlikely that Heydrich did.

Despite the occasional friction and fundamentally different approaches to the world, the two men developed a remarkable working harmony based on furthering their shared consuming ambition. Their drive to surpass others had brought them together in a way that made them indispensable to each other. Their partnership met an early test with the Nazis' advent to power in January of 1933. While the Weimar Republic tottered and vicious struggles for power raged among the party leaders in Berlin, faraway Munich was quiet, its leading Nazis left out of the dispensations of Chancellor Hitler. Bavaria was even showing signs of resisting the new order until it was brought to heel on March 9 with a command from Berlin to appoint a Nazi governor. The telegram was delivered to the state chancellery in Munich at pistolpoint by Heydrich, backed by an SS detachment.

Only then did the Bavarian Nazis get their chance. Adolf Wagner, the

gauleiter, or party chairman for the state, became minister of the interior. Himmler was named police commissioner of Munich (with Heydrich taking over the political department), and a month later Himmler became commander of the Bavarian political police (with Heydrich as his deputy). These were minor posts, far from the center of action, but the two functionaries were determined to make the most of them. "How tragic," said Himmler speciously, "that my new duties will bring me into contact only with the lowest species of humanity, with criminals, Jews, and enemies of the state, when all my thoughts and endeavors are for the elite of our race. But the Führer has assigned this duty to me. I shall not shirk it." Fortunately for Himmler's sense of duty, his assistant Heydrich had readied a program of reorganization that would completely change the role of the police.

The night of Bavaria's capitulation to nazification, Himmler's SS and Ernst Röhm's SA, armed now with the powers of the state and guided by Heydrich's SD operatives with their index cards, fanned out to establish their rule. By presidential decree, police had received the power to search homes, confiscate property, and arrest suspected enemies of the state, all without the formality of a court order or court review. The rationalization for these emergency powers was the supposed threat of communist violence, of which the Reichstag fire in February was held up as the most dangerous example.

Indeed, in Bavaria as elsewhere in the Reich, the communists were the first to feel the effects of what became known as "preventive detention." But they were only the first of many. After the arrest of virtually every communist activist in Bavaria, Heydrich continued pulling cards and sending out squads—for socialists,

Berlin police obeying orders from the Nazi regime collar two suspects. Such scenes were common in 1933 after Prussian Interior Minister Hermann Göring called for a roundup of communists and socialists.

for trade unionists, and then for Catholic politicians. Himmler meanwhile pleaded with Berlin for more money to finance the "spadework" necessary to start the compilation of even more indexes. "The central Bavarian card index of foreign citizens, which is to be newly made," he wrote, "necessitates the writing of some 200,000 index cards."

As a result of these sweeps, the prisons of Bavaria were soon filled,

Prisoners arrested during the crackdown on leftists and other targeted groups exercise in the courtyard of a Bavarian jail in April 1933. The suspects were told only that they were being taken into "protective custody."

prompting Interior Minister Wagner to offer a suggestion dripping with irony: "I recommend using the methods that were formerly employed with regard to mass arrests of members of the National Socialist German Workers' party. It will be recalled that they were locked in any old hovel, and no one cared if the prisoners were exposed to the weather or not." Within a fortnight of his proposal, a stockade was thrown up around an unused munitions factory at nearby Dachau, and Bavaria had its first concentration camp—with a capacity, Himmler announced, of 5,000 inmates.

Under this onslaught—Heydrich boasted of 16,409 arrests by the end of 1933—opposition to the Nazi hold on Bavaria wilted. Although many alleged enemies of the state were not detained for long (Heydrich reported 12,544 people released from custody in the same nine-month period), the fright and the humiliation of the experience was usually enough to demoralize and intimidate the internees utterly.

The lists of enemies continued to grow, and people continued to disappear—now clergy, journalists, and so-called reactionaries. One Louis Strassner, owner of a shoe factory, was hauled off because he paid his workers less than the standard rate and rejected Nazi coercion on the subject by saying that he was master of his own factory. Exercising such arbitrary power over the population of Bavaria was a heady experience for Himmler and Heydrich, but local power was not enough. If chance had decreed that they be police, then they must be supreme police. "Now the SS should penetrate the police and form a new organization within it," said Heydrich. And Himmler stated the vision even more boldly: "A nationwide police force," he declared, "is the strongest linchpin that a state can have."

Germany had no lack of police. Each state and larger city had its own force, with uniformed personnel handling patrol and protection duties and plain-clothes divisions conducting criminal and political investigations. The official attitude toward political police was ambivalent. They had ceased to function after the 1918 revolution, but the new government soon

Politicizing the Police Officer

A patrolman conducts traffic in Munich, birthplace of SS power.

Demonstrating their Nazi loyalty in a swastika formation, police at a 1934 Berlin sports festival fire a volley.

"Every bullet that leaves the barrel of a police pistol now is my bullet," declared Hermann Göring in February 1933 as his Prussian police relentlessly cracked down on leftists. "If one calls this murder, then I have murdered."

Göring was the first official of the Third Reich to assert personal authority over the police, but it remained for Himmler and Heydrich to realize that ambition on a national scale. They did so without Göring's ostentation, making sure that Hitler was duly honored as high commissioner of the emerging police state. When the Führer watched his goose-stepping police pass on parade *(below)*, he could safely conclude that their weapons were his weapons. Yet effective control over this huge civil force and its diverse personnel—from the uniformed officer directing city traffic to the plain-clothes Gestapo agent lurking in the crowd—rested with the leaders of the SS.

Hitler reviews marching policemen in the late 1930s. Such military drill long had been part of German police training.

felt as threatened internally as had the old, and surveillants of political opponents were reintroduced to police departments everywhere. These were local organizations, however, and not under federal control.

Himmler and Heydrich considered this unsatisfactory. If the party was to consolidate its power and move unchallenged toward its goals, it must first get a firm grip on the country's police and then make better use of the power latent in the multitude of police organizations. Himmler and Heydrich intended to show the way in Bavaria by gaining control of the local political police forces, separating them from the regular police, and forging them into a statewide organization. Heydrich had prepared exhaustively for the eventual seizure of power, and even as the SS squads were making their relentless calls, he and Himmler were converting the political police of Munich, then of Bavaria, into an enlarged instrument of terror.

First the politically unreliable and incompetent police officers had to go; Heydrich knew who they were and fired them. Then well-trained professionals were put in charge of every operation; Heydrich had the names of the potential recruits in his copious card files. He knew better than to try to fill all his posts with Nazis; there were not enough competent ones to go around, and he was determined not to hire what he called "the blockheads the party normally made use of." He was confident he could find the individuals he needed among some of the Nazis' former enemies—both policemen and academics. This paradoxical expectation was confirmed when he called in such professional Nazi hunters as Franz Josef Huber and his colleague in the Bavarian political police, Inspector Heinrich Müller, whose specialty was hunting communists. Heydrich frightened such men half to death, redirected their fear into fervor, and saw them plunge enthusiastically into their new work on behalf of the National Socialists.

Next Heydrich reached not only beyond the party—neither Huber nor Müller was a member—but beyond the police fraternity as well. Heydrich had long been an admirer of the British secret service. He saw it as a stellar collection of intellectuals who were devoted to their country, and he believed it had performed far better than German intelligence agencies. This he was determined to change, and from the earliest days of his SD he actively recruited what passed for intellectuals in the Nazi world. Academic degrees in law, economics, engineering, or bookkeeping counted for more with Heydrich than credentials in the Nazi party. The party was important, of course—not only because Himmler worshiped its ideals, but because it was a useful lever with which to pry the political police from the restraints of civil government and legal precedent.

Himmler and Heydrich intended to obey no man but Hitler and no law whatsoever. That first became obvious in the matter of the concentration

Conducting a random check, plain-clothes police officers halt a pedestrian to inspect his identification papers. Everyone in Nazi Germany was required to carry proof of identity.

camps. Unlike the SA rowdies in Berlin, who did not care if the shots and screams from their holding pens were heard, Himmler was fastidious about keeping word of his camps from the public. Nevertheless, tales of torture and death soon spread, especially from Dachau. This created a problem.

Beginning in May of 1933, Munich's public prosecutor investigated case after case of suspicious death at Dachau, usually finding that torture and beatings had been the cause. Late that year he brought formal charges of incitement to murder against the three top officials at Dachau. Himmler was forced to dismiss the camp commandant. Highly irritated, Himmler asked Adolf Wagner to propose that the Bavarian cabinet ban future investigations of concentration camps "for reasons of state policy." But it was not yet the policy of the state to see no evil; the cabinet refused to exempt the camps from the law. Himmler had other means to his ends, however. He offered the snappy black uniform of an SS officer to the senior state attorney in Bavaria, Walther Stepp. Although Stepp was a Nazi, he had supported the investigations. Himmler assured him that with his new rank he would be better equipped to deal with any problems at Dachau, and Stepp accepted. Within a year he had become deputy chief of the Bavarian political police. Henceforth, fewer voices were raised in protest, and the wholesale arrests, beatings, and murders continued.

Himmler chose Theodor Eicke as the new commandant of Dachau. Eicke, a fanatical SS officer, was known for his violent methods but also regarded as a skilled recruiter and organizer. To help meet the need for camp guards, Himmler and Eicke created a new SS formation, the Death's-

Head unit, whose members were granted the right to wear the skull and crossbones on their collar patches.

Thus, by early 1934 Himmler and Heydrich had subjugated a major German state with a meticulously planned and ruthlessly executed assault. Heydrich, moreover, had tested the procedures and created the nucleus of a national police force. Just as his SD had been ready to move against Bavaria, his political police were now capable of taking on the German nation. But the way was blocked by another Nazi official who had both similar ambitions and an earlier start toward realizing them. This was Hermann Göring, who was more intimate than Himmler with Adolf Hitler —and thus more influential in the party—and who exercised his power in Prussia, which included the national capital of Berlin and was the only state larger than Bavaria.

Göring had received ministerial duties in the national and Prussian governments in January of 1933, several weeks before the nazification of Bavaria. As interior minister of Prussia, he was responsible for policing the capital and two-thirds of the land area of Germany. Like Himmler and Heydrich, he soon recognized that in the Nazis' world of intrigue, untrammeled police power would be decisive. He gave it his full attention but had to move with care. Many of his regular police officials either were members of the SA and loyal to Röhm or belonged to the SS. (Göring's chief of the Prussian police, Kurt Daluege, was an SS major general.) Nor was he oblivious to the fact that the Bavarian duo represented a serious threat to his aspirations: "Himmler and Heydrich will never get to Berlin," he vowed.

Göring moved swiftly to separate the Prussian political police from the rest of the state police organization. The political arm was assigned to a man without any party connection, Rudolf Diels, a senior civil servant in the Prussian Interior Ministry. Like Göring, Diels had a ready appetite for the good life but was also an effective administrator. Göring authorized the political police in Berlin to disregard the restrictions imposed by state law. He moved them out of police headquarters and into their own establishment, at an address that was soon to become infamous: 8 Prinz Albrechtstrasse. Next he created a statewide agency that absorbed the political police throughout Prussia. This was done, it was explained in a memorandum, "in the interests of uniform higher direction of the political police." Göring named the new force the Geheime Staatspolizeiamt, or Secret State Police Office. A postal clerk responsible for abbreviating the name for a franking stamp contributed to the language of fear when he

This aluminum skull-and-crossbones cap insignia was worn by all SS units—including the aptly named *Totenkopf-verbände,* or Death's-Head detachments, that ran the concentration camps.

Theodor Eicke, commandant of Dachau, enjoined his guards to live up to their death's-head symbol by treating prisoners with "inflexible harshness."

In 1936 Himmler *(center)* and Rudolf Hess *(without hat)* examine the model for an enlarged concentration camp at Dachau. Its renovation and the opening of camps at Sachsenhausen in 1936 and Buchenwald in 1937 signaled SS determination to make preventive detention a permanent weapon.

dubbed the organization the Gestapa, soon popularly modified to Gestapo.

By the 1933 election campaign, Göring had a firm grip on the largest police force in Germany, and he launched it at opponents of the new order with glee. Having removed the police from almost all legal restraints, he declared 50,000 members of the SA and the SS to be auxiliary police so they could join the hunt. "I have no obligation to abide by the law," he exulted. "My job is simply to annihilate and exterminate—nothing more."

Thus encouraged, the deputized thugs of the SA indulged in an orgy of mayhem so grotesque that it offended the sensibilities even of men long accustomed to the casual use of violence. Roving gangs dragged people from their homes and off the streets, jamming bewildered prisoners by the hundreds into improvised detention centers—fifty of them in Berlin alone. There the prisoners were treated brutally. Even Göring was appalled by what he had wrought, especially when he found he could not control it. The SA was too unruly and commanded the loyalty of too many of his own police officers; all he could do, he decided, was ride it out.

Diels, on the other hand, went to war against the extremists. Neither a Nazi nor a brute, he set his political police on the trail of the torturers, tracked them down, and forced them to release their prisoners. On one occasion his men, armed with machine guns, surrounded an SA detention center in Berlin and forced the Brownshirts to surrender. Diels was revolted by what he found inside: prisoners who had been savagely and methodically beaten, "a dozen or so thugs being employed in fifteen-minute shifts to belabor their victims with iron bars, rubber truncheons, and whips. When we entered, these living skeletons were lying in rows on filthy straw with festering wounds."

Göring allowed Diels to mitigate the worst of the Brownshirt excesses but, wary of SA power, gave him no overt support. Meanwhile, elements of the SS who had worked their way into Göring's Gestapo and whose organization had scattered its own less visible torture chambers throughout

Germany, campaigned viciously for the downfall of Diels and his faction. "We were living in a den of murderers," wrote one Gestapo official, Hans Bernd Gisevius. He recalled that State Chief of Criminal Police Arthur Nebe developed the habit of entering and leaving his office "by the rear staircase, with his hand always resting on the cocked automatic in his pocket. It was so usual for members of the Gestapo to arrest one another that we scarcely took notice of such incidents."

In one typical sequence, an SS squad raided Diels's home while he was away, locked his wife in a bedroom, and searched the apartment in vain for evidence of communist sympathies. It did not take the Gestapo chief long to identify and arrest the man who had led the raid. But Göring, under pressure from all sides, listened to Himmler's howls of protest and ordered the man released to the SS for trial. Diels took the decision as a death sentence and fled to Czechoslovakia. Within a month, however—apparently after threatening to reveal embarrassing information about Göring—Diels was back in charge of the Gestapo, and the briefly triumphant SS loyalists there were afraid for their lives. The night after Diels's return, Gisevius hid in a hotel room, then joined Nebe in Police Chief Daluege's office to discuss their predicament. A subordinate suggested inviting Diels to a meeting and throwing him out a window. Instead, the antagonists eventually made a peace of sorts and went on with their work.

Despite this internal tumult, the Gestapo continued to identify and round up increasing numbers of public enemies, and the buoyant Göring remained firmly in overall charge, at least within Prussia. But the Nazis were bent on destroying the power of the state governments, not building it as Göring was doing, and on that count he faced a serious challenge on the national level. The Reich interior minister, Wilhelm Frick, sought in late 1933 to integrate the German states and take command of their police organizations, only to be outmaneuvered by Göring. Before Frick was able to act, Göring removed the Prussian secret police from the state interior ministry and made it an independent force responsible to himself. Frick, a former follower of Gregor Strasser, did not have sufficient weight in party affairs to challenge Göring directly, so he allied himself with Himmler.

With Frick's support, Himmler took over the political police of state after state, until only Prussia and little Schaumburg-Lippe remained out of his reach. Göring stood fast for a time in Prussia, and he might have frustrated the plan entirely were it not for his growing dread of the SA. The Brownshirts were three million strong, thirty times the size of the Reichswehr; they were hungry for power and eager to trample anyone, Nazi or not, who stood in their way. Increasingly, they muttered that Hitler himself—along with his cronies, of course—was the one betraying them. The menacing

In April of 1934 Himmler and Göring seal the pact giving Himmler control of the Prussian secret police, known as the Gestapo. The name was subsequently applied to the national secret police force organized by Himmler and Heydrich, and *Gestapo* became a synonym for terror throughout Germany.

presence of the SA finally persuaded Göring to compromise. He ousted his protégé Diels, this time for good, and on April 20, 1934, named Himmler to supervise the Prussian Gestapo. Two days later, Himmler appointed Heydrich his second in command. The trio's first cooperative venture, the Blood Purge in June and July that decapitated the SA, was a success.

The instrument of intimidation that had been cast during the first encounter of Heydrich and Himmler, forged in the poverty-stricken years of struggle as the SD, and honed during a season of terror in Bavaria was now to be wielded against all of Germany. Once more, Heydrich was ready with his corps of assistants and his boxes of card files. Only now, with control of the Gestapo, his resources were vastly greater. The Gestapo had begun with a staff of 35; by early 1935 it employed 607. Heydrich tightened its organization even as he expanded it, imparting to everything a military style of procedure. At the same time, he put loyalists in every key position.

One of Heydrich's favorite intellectuals, Werner Best, became chief of the division that handled administration and law. An elegant thirty-year-old attorney from Darmstadt, Best soon established himself as the legal apologist for the Gestapo. He was ever ready with convoluted but smoothly stated arguments whose conclusions were the same: that it was legal to ignore the law as long as rules laid down by the leadership were followed.

Heydrich paid close attention to the two Gestapo operational divisions, counterespionage and internal investigations. He installed the former Munich police inspectors Franz Josef Huber and Heinrich Müller as section chiefs in the internal branch, Huber to prosecute reactionaries and Müller to continue hunting left-wing radicals. Another section chief was assigned to watch members of the party for signs of heresy.

The bureaucracy of terror soon functioned as smoothly in Prussia and the rest of Germany as it had for some time in Bavaria. The card files continued to proliferate. Under *A* in the index, for example, listing dangerous enemies of the state, colored tabs on the left side of the cards indicated whether an individual was marked for arrest immediately prior to mobilization for war (red), for arrest after mobilization was announced (blue), or merely for close surveillance (green). Similar tabs on the right-hand side signaled classifications of the enemy: communist (dark red), Marxist (light red), assassin (brown), or grumbler (violet).

As the size, cost, and power of the Gestapo doubled and redoubled under Heydrich, he found it necessary to justify his efforts. There were those in the party who believed that after the Blood Purge, after the thousands of arrests, with every opposition party in shambles and Nazi power virtually absolute throughout Germany, it should be possible to ease up a little.

Such notions were dangerous to Heydrich's ambitions, and he confronted them publicly. Although "enemy organizations have been smashed," he declared in a rare 1935 speech, the threat they posed remained. The foe had simply become invisible and was therefore all the more perilous. Sinister forces—"world Jewry, world Freemasonry, and the clergy, who are to a large extent political"—had coordinated a massive attack on Hitler's Germany. And the unspoken assumption Heydrich encouraged with this was that only an unfettered Gestapo, under his leadership, could deal with these forces of evil.

The tactic worked. A handful of courageous public prosecutors, judges, and lawyers spoke out for legal process and against the abuses of the concentration camps. But they were ignored by those who held the ultimate power, and the twin juggernauts of the Gestapo and the SD rolled

Gestapo agents, who dressed in civilian clothes, carried identification badges such as this. The obverse bears the agent's number and the full name of the Gestapo—the Geheime Staatspolizei, or Secret State Police; on the reverse, a German eagle perches on a wreath encircling a swastika.

onward. Fear became pervasive. "Soon no one dared to utter anything that might be construed as hostile to the regime or even critical of it," recalled Bernt Engelmann, who was a teenager in Berlin in 1934. "No one knew whether there might not be an SD spy among his close friends or even in his own family." A friend of the Engelmanns, a widow named Meinzerhagen, tried out a new radio one night, turning the dial to see what stations it brought in. Her apartment windows were closed, her drapes drawn, only her daughter was present. Yet she found herself in short order under interrogation by Gestapo agents, charged with listening to "nigger jazz" and "horror stories about Germany" on foreign broadcasts. Only her next-door neighbor, who had once complained about her beating carpets during his afternoon nap, could have denounced her.

Meinzerhagen got off with a warning, but not all such trivial denunciations had trivial results. Engelmann remembered the New Year's Eve celebration that year at which he and his parents shared a table with a group of close friends. After dinner and dancing, "the mood became quite exuberant, and at midnight people drank to each other, clinked glasses, and wished one another a Happy New Year. As people kissed, the lights in the room were switched off for a moment. When the lights came back on, the noise suddenly died away. A heavy, wheezing man in a brown party uniform with an extra-wide leather cross-strap and brown riding boots clambered up onto the podium to make a speech." After a long boozy regurgitation of stock Nazi phrases, the man concluded with a ringing "God save our Führer!"—to which an elderly attorney at the Engelmanns' table quietly responded, for only his friends to hear, "And us from him!" A few days later, the attorney was arrested by the Gestapo, branded a "dangerous enemy of the state," and consigned to a concentration camp. Shortly after that, his family received an urn containing his ashes.

Even some dedicated, high-ranking Nazis were appalled by the denial of fundamental justice and basic human rights in the concentration camps. In the summer of 1934, the Reich minister of justice, Franz Gürtner, and the party's ranking legal expert, Hans Frank, appealed directly to Hitler. While Himmler stared from his place at the Führer's side, the lawyers proposed that the camps be done away with and those persons already in custody be dealt with by regular courts of law. Hitler's response was cryptic. Such steps, he said, would be "premature." The meeting was over.

Protests were the exception, and they became even rarer after Hitler indicated that he was no more concerned with concepts of law or human rights than were Himmler and Heydrich. Many German lawyers—and indeed many judges—soon accepted the principle defined by the Gestapo's Werner Best: "Insofar as the police are acting in accordance with the

In an early example of anti-Semitic activity under Hitler, Nazis picketing a Jewish-owned store in Berlin in April 1933 wear placards urging passersby not to buy from Jews; a comrade is poised to photograph customers entering the store.

rules laid down by their superiors—right up to the highest level—they can never be acting 'lawlessly' or 'contrary to the law'." The abuses continued. In Bavaria, the political police carried out Wagner's directive to "arrest without pity all persons strolling about in a suspicious manner." In Prussia in 1935 and 1936 the Gestapo arrested 7,000 people whose crime, as defined by Best, was to make "any attempt to gain recognition for, or even to uphold, different political ideas."

"It is enough to drive one to despair," lamented Justice Minister Gürtner. By 1936, however, there were few officials left who would agree with him openly. Their number included Reich Interior Minister Frick, who was concerned less with the lawlessness of the Gestapo than with his loss of control over it. Diels, the former head of the Gestapo, continued to oppose its excesses, as did a handful of SS officers and ranking civil administrators. Mixed as their motives were, these opponents shared a fervent desire to stop the accumulation of power by Himmler and Heydrich. Since the movement toward a single national police force was clearly irreversible, the dissenters decided to support it, provided that the force was placed under the Interior Ministry's control. For his own reasons, Himmler was ready to negotiate with his opponents, and in February of 1936 he agreed to a law making Gestapo offices subordinate to individual state governments.

Encouraged by this apparent victory, Frick drafted a decree stipulating that all of the national police would come under the Interior Ministry and that Himmler would become inspector of the Gestapo, reporting to Frick. Heydrich took charge of the staff negotiations between the ministry and the SS, and he adopted a very hard line: The draft must be changed to award Himmler ministerial rank in the national government and the title chief of the German police, in addition to Reichsführer of the SS. Frick objected to Hitler, only to find that his apparent victory had been hollow; he had in fact been completely outmaneuvered. Hitler gave him a crumb of a concession—Himmler would not receive ministerial rank—but on most other counts Frick was overruled. On June 17, 1936, Himmler was named chief of all German police. Henceforth the SS, its information-gathering SD, the various state political police agencies, including the Gestapo, and all the uniformed and criminal police in Germany would be under the control of one man, Himmler, who now answered only to one other man, Adolf Hitler.

Heydrich, of course, immediately became head of the department supervising all political and criminal police. Characteristically, he was ready to expand the scale of his card-file methods. The SD and the secret and criminal police, he decreed, would work together toward "the complete apprehension of opponents" and "the systematic control, destruction, crippling, and elimination of these opponents by means of executive force." Heydrich's catalog of enemies had continued to grow. The categories were listed in a 1937 internal memorandum: "communism, Marxism, Jewry, the politically active churches, Freemasonry, political malcontents (grumblers), the nationalist opposition, reactionaries, economic saboteurs, habitual criminals, also abortionists and homosexuals (who from the point of view of population policy are prejudicial to the strength of the people and defense; with homosexuals there is also the danger of espionage), traitors to the country and the state."

Ready as Heydrich was to move against this array of opponents, he had an irritating technicality to overcome with respect to the criminal element. Except under court order, the tenuous—but in Heydrich's hands entirely sufficient—legal basis for preventive detention of enemies of the state did not exist for ordinary criminals. Heydrich ordered Best to devise a complicated legal argument to show that here, too, the police could ignore the law. With that taken care of, the Criminal Police fanned out across Germany early in 1937 to arrest 2,000 habitual "offenders against morality" and "antisocial malefactors" and incarcerated them in concentration camps.

This was the final step in Germany's conversion from a republic ruled by law to a police state. The police were removed from the control of local governments and courts and told that they need not abide by the law or respect human rights; now their mission was transformed from defensive to offensive. No longer were they responsible for protecting citizens and tracking down offenders for judgment by the courts. Instead, they were charged with protecting the state—against its citizens, if necessary—by pursuing people who might commit an offense in the future. The police would decide who deserved to be arrested, and the commandants of the concentration camps would decide on the severity of their punishment.

Yet neither Himmler nor Heydrich was satisfied, and more than insatiable ambition drove them on; in the maelstrom of Hitler's government, littered with organizations and alliances created and abandoned in the

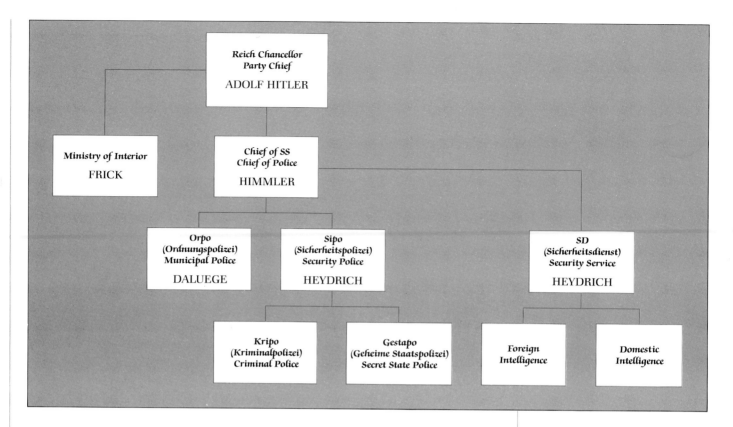

			Reich Chancellor Party Chief ADOLF HITLER		
Ministry of Interior FRICK		**Chief of SS Chief of Police** HIMMLER			
	Orpo (Ordnungspolizei) Municipal Police DALUEGE	**Sipo** (Sicherheitspolizei) Security Police HEYDRICH		**SD** (Sicherheitsdienst) Security Service HEYDRICH	
	Kripo (Kriminalpolizei) Criminal Police	**Gestapo** (Geheime Staatspolizei) Secret State Police	**Foreign Intelligence**	**Domestic Intelligence**	

quest for more power, to stand still was to be consumed. By Hitler's deliberate design, everyone was pitted against everyone else. Partnerships were temporary, principles did not exist, and nothing was prohibited except what displeased the Führer. The path to success had been demonstrated: Find enemies, destroy them, seize their power, keep moving.

Heydrich found himself the master of an enlarged but still-divided kingdom—the Gestapo, the Criminal Police, and the SD. The SD had slipped into the shadows while Heydrich was distracted by other more glittering duties, but it was still the official intelligence agency for the Nazi party. And in the new police state the SD had planted a network of informers and spies so dense that it seemed the slightest lapse by the most insignificant German was recorded immediately on an index card somewhere. But the SD envied the power of the Gestapo, and the Gestapo resented the constant interference of the SD. By 1937, they were expending a great deal of energy competing with each other.

Heydrich had a special resentment of his own: He felt he should not have to consign his thousands of prisoners to Eicke and the Death's-Head units for punishment. Eicke, the commandant of Dachau and the executioner of Röhm, had been promoted by Himmler to inspector of all the proliferating concentration camps in Germany. Under Himmler's supervision, Eicke had reorganized the sprawling system into just four large camps—Dachau, Buchenwald, Sachsenhausen, and Lichtenburg.

Although Heydrich had his hands full with the continuing mass arrests and the increasing number of catfights among his agencies, he campaigned to bring down Eicke and seize yet another fiefdom. Suddenly Heydrich became concerned about the mistreatment of prisoners, and he began to report to Himmler a litany of abuses. The camps should be turned over to him, Heydrich argued. He did not intend to treat the prisoners more

The chart above shows how security operations were organized in the Third Reich. In 1936 Hitler appointed Himmler chief of all German police, effectively removing Interior Minister Wilhelm Frick from the chain of command. Himmler, in turn, delegated control of his vast domain to two avid subordinates: Kurt Daluege, head of the Municipal Police (ORPO), and Reinhard Heydrich, who had several assignments. As head of the Security Police (SIPO), he oversaw both the investigation of conventional offenders by the Criminal Police (KRIPO) and the tracking down of so-called enemies of the state by the Gestapo. Simultaneously, Heydrich ran two SD intelligence services, one foreign, the other domestic.

humanely, just more efficiently. Himmler, however, refused to give in. Like his Führer, Himmler believed in playing his subordinates off against each other, thus preventing any of them from becoming powerful enough to challenge him. As long as he kept the bulldog Eicke in the pit with Heydrich, they would be too busy savaging each other to plot against him.

Himmler had other problems. He was now the head of two important, separate organizations—the SS and the national police. But the police, by far the most powerful and intrusive agency in the lives of the German people, consisted of individuals who were not racially screened, not trained in Himmler's beloved Germanic folklore or the virtues of the peasantry. He was not content to have the police dominated by the SS; he wanted them to be absorbed by the SS. Hitler, however, saw no reason for Himmler to become that powerful. Nor did Göring, who had his own thoughts on the rightful identity of the second most powerful official of the Reich. Hitler kept Himmler and Göring in the pit together.

Even Hitler, supreme dictator though he was, chafed at certain limitations. His problem was the army, which was resisting his plans for foreign expansion. In November of 1937 Hitler announced to his senior military staff that within six years he intended to solve the problem of living space for the German people, even at the risk of war. His first targets, he declared, were Austria and Czechoslovakia. The war minister, Field Marshal Werner von Blomberg, and the commander in chief of the army, Colonel General Werner Freiherr von Fritsch, threw up their hands and regaled the Führer with reasons why his design was impossible.

Hitler had not eviscerated the army as he had every other institution in Germany capable of giving him trouble. The army had weapons, making it a dangerous adversary. It also had a long tradition of imposing its own brand of order and honor on German politics when necessary, and Hitler did not want to trigger that reaction. Moreover, the army so far had been more often an ally than an obstacle. Instead of resisting Hitler's seizure of power, the army stood by while democracy was snuffed out, even providing the transportation for Hitler's assassins during the Blood Purge in 1934.

Now, however, Hitler was beginning to regard the army's lack of enthusiasm as a threat to his plans. But he did not dare to sack its senior officers without cause, lest the army turn on him. Meanwhile, Himmler, frustrated by the incomplete SS domination of the police, groped for a way to please the Führer sufficiently to win another prize. And Heydrich, galled by the independence of the concentration camps, schemed to push his mentor up another notch in the Nazi hierarchy and pry Eicke from under Himmler's protection. Then, only a few days after Hitler's unsatisfactory meeting with his top soldiers, someone remembered a report that was gathering dust in a Gestapo file. The dossier promised to solve everyone's problem.

The previous year, Otto Schmidt, a convicted thief and blackmailer, claimed to have witnessed a homosexual liaison involving an army officer named Fritsch. Later, Schmidt had been encouraged to identify one of the transgressors as General Fritsch, commander in chief of the army. Himmler reportedly had taken the matter to Hitler, who glanced at the transcript of the Schmidt interrogation, labeled it "muck," and curtly ordered Himmler to burn it. Fritsch at that time was considered indispensable to Germany's rearmament efforts and therefore enjoyed Hitler's total support.

Of course, the "muck" had not been burned but filed, and with Fritsch no longer deemed indispensable, the information was retrieved and the case reopened. Gestapo agents began tailing the army commander and investigating his life for signs of homosexuality. They found none, nor could they corroborate Schmidt's statement—but they persevered. Then, in January of 1938, they stumbled over something else. War Minister Blomberg, a widower, that month married an attractive government secretary in a private ceremony attended by Hitler and Göring. Within days the Criminal Police in Berlin discovered that the new Frau Blomberg was a former prostitute, and they assembled a collection of obscene photographs of her.

Göring knew about both cases because of his role as nominal head of the Prussian Gestapo, and he began plying a new thought. If both the army commander in chief and the war minister were ruined, he reasoned, surely he would end up in command of the armed forces. On the night of January 24, Göring took the two files to Hitler. The case against Frau Blomberg was conclusive and the resignation of the war minister a foregone conclusion. Moreover, Hitler now accepted at face value the case against Fritsch that he had previously termed "muck."

Gestapo headquarters (*below*), at 8 Prinz Albrechtstrasse in Berlin, was the epicenter of a secret-police apparatus that at its peak employed 20,000 agents.

Hitler's reaction was swift—though not quite what Göring had expected. He dismissed Blomberg and forced Fritsch to retire. (Fritsch was so shocked by the accusation that all he could do was shout, "It's a stinking lie!") In the same sweep, Hitler relieved sixteen other generals of their

In Gestapo headquarters this teletype room provided instant communication with sixty-two offices. Field agents relayed news about suspected subversives from well-placed informants, including block wardens who spied on their neighbors.

Himmler convenes a meeting at Gestapo headquarters in 1941. From right to left are Gestapo chief Heinrich Müller; Heydrich; Himmler; Franz Huber, one of Heydrich's early recruits; and Arthur Nebe, head of the Criminal Police.

commands, reassigned forty-four more, replaced his foreign minister, and disbanded the War Ministry altogether. In its place he created the High Command of the Armed Forces—to be known by its initials, OKW. Its commander in chief was not Göring but Hitler. Lack of enthusiasm for military adventures was no longer a problem. In March Hitler sent the German army into Austria and without opposition annexed it as a new German state. In October, having faced down the western Allies at Munich, he occupied 10,000 square miles of Czechoslovakia. He had achieved the first stages of his plan for territorial expansion without triggering a war.

Meanwhile, the frustrations of Himmler and Heydrich remained unresolved. In fact, soon after the sacking of the army high command, their fortunes took a wrenching turn for the worse. Fritsch, his career and reputation at stake, refused to leave office gracefully and forced a full court-martial to try the charge against him. Confident of acquittal, he submitted to Gestapo interrogation before the trial. During one of these sessions, Himmler assembled twelve SS officers in the next room and ordered them to exert their mental powers on Fritsch to make him tell the truth. Walter Schellenberg, an assistant to Heydrich, walked in on the séance and saw the officers "sitting in a circle, all sunk in deep and silent contemplation." It was, he wrote later, "a remarkable sight."

During preparations for the trial, it became apparent that the case was one of mistaken identity. The liaison reported by Schmidt had involved a Captain Frisch, no relation to the former commanding officer of the army. Desperately, Heydrich and Himmler tried to keep the revelation secret, even from Göring—who had been promoted to field marshal and appointed president of Fritsch's court-martial. Word leaked out, however, and fear of reprisal from the army spread like poison gas through Gestapo headquarters in Berlin. On the evening before the court was to convene, Heydrich invited Schellenberg to join him for dinner in his office—and to bring a loaded pistol. Schellenberg had been hired as an intellectual, not a gunman, but he had a reputation as a marksman, which Heydrich anxiously confirmed. Then the mystified Schellenberg was treated to a strange, intimate meal with an increasingly nervous Heydrich. Hours passed, and at length Heydrich tensely consulted a clock and said, "If they don't start marching from Potsdam during the next hour and a half, the danger will have passed." Only then did Heydrich reveal that certain army officers had considered attacking Gestapo headquarters with armed troops.

The army did not march that night. But Göring learned the truth about the Fritsch case; in the courtroom the field marshal bullied Schmidt into admitting his perjury and led the court-martial to a verdict of "innocent on all counts." Now both Heydrich and Himmler—who was furious about

Honeymooning in Java in May 1938 after he was forced to step down as war minister, Werner von Blomberg stands by his disgraced wife, Erna, whose record as a prostitute was uncovered by Arthur Nebe's Criminal Police. When compromising photographs of the bride reached Nebe's desk, he recalled that Hitler had attended the wedding and exclaimed, "Good God, this woman has kissed the Führer's hand!"

having been let down by his trusted subordinate—trembled anew with anticipation of a punitive strike. But the army contented itself with Fritsch's reinstatement and public exoneration. He was given command of a regiment and the following year would die leading it in combat. Himmler, meanwhile, had the false witness Schmidt taken out and shot.

The Fritsch affair nearly ended the Himmler-Heydrich partnership. Himmler said in public that he had been misled by incompetent subordinates, and while Heydrich was not among those fired or transferred as a result, his culpability was unmistakable. His method of atonement was to struggle again to reorganize the German police under the SS, as Himmler wanted, and to gain control of the concentration camps, as he wanted.

Heydrich and Himmler salvaged their partnership and in fall 1939 managed a reorganization that gave them advantages on paper but few in fact. It created the Reich Central Security Office, or RSHA, which combined all police functions and the SS. The organization was riddled with conflicting loyalties—some departments reporting to the party, some to civil-service authorities, some to the SS—and warring personalities. But it was the best the two schemers could do, and in any case they had seized new opportunities. On September 1 the Germans had marched into Poland. ✚

Silently defiant, prisoners
at the Sachsenhausen camp
outside Berlin stand at attention
as a uniformed SS man calls
the morning roll.

His machine gun at the ready, an ▷
SS guard in one of Dachau's
watchtowers keeps an eye on
inmates laboring in the fields.

The First Concentration Camps

Shortly after Adolf Hitler's elevation to chancellor in January of 1933, scores of crude prison compounds sprang up across Germany. These were the first of the concentration camps that would become permanent, frightening features of life under nazism. Into their maw trudged thousands of communists and other political foes of the new regime, all summarily jailed under a decree that allowed the SS, SA, and regular police to incarcerate anyone suspected of being an "enemy of the state." No trial was necessary.

Most of the early compounds—dubbed "wild camps" because control by the government or any outside agency was so minimal—were run by brown-shirted SA thugs. Within a year, however, Heinrich Himmler and the SS had taken over, consolidating and organizing the system. The first SS installation was located near the Bavarian town of Dachau. The camp's barbed-wire fences and harsh rules became models for Buchenwald, Sachsenhausen, and the other prisons that followed. All were designed, as one survivor recalled, to crush "every trace of actual or potential opposition to Nazi rule. Segregation, debasement, humiliation, extermination—these were the effective forms of terror."

Rounding Up Victims of All Kinds

Himmler and his cohorts sent diverse groups of Germans to concentration camps between 1933 and 1939. To the 26,000 so-called political criminals were soon added the dregs of the underworld, as the SS jailed thousands of habitual lawbreakers. Also picked up were "subversives," anyone the spies of the SS, SD, and Gestapo denounced for uttering the mildest criticism of Hitler's regime. Then came a bizarre mixture of people whom Himmler considered "antisocial malefactors"—tramps, gypsies, prostitutes, homosexuals, even Freemasons and pacifist Jehovah's Witnesses.

In 1938 about 35,000 Jews were imprisoned, just for being Jews. They were released only if they promised to emigrate—and leave behind whatever wealth they had.

In a Berlin cellar in 1933, a Storm Trooper guards communists who will be shipped without trial to a new prison camp.

Forced to perform a mock welcoming ceremony, Dürrgoy-Breslau inmates greet a prisoner, Reichstag President Paul Löbe.

Rules and a Regimen That Could Kill

"Forget your wives and children. Here you will die like dogs," an SS camp commander proclaimed to every batch of male arrivals. The threat was not far from the truth. Prisoners worked at least eleven hours a day, six days a week, a regimen that combined with meager food and poor sanitation to kill thousands of inmates.

Punishment for imperfect behavior was cruel and sometimes fatal. Mild offenses such as stealing a cigarette brought twenty-five lashes. For more serious infractions, such as being late for roll call, the penalty was solitary confinement in total darkness, an isolation that drove some prisoners insane. Execution was specified for many so-called crimes, such as being an agitator— that is, talking politics.

Inmates wearing homemade prison stripes dig a trench at Dachau in 1938. Such work gangs often were supervised by prisoner-foremen who held their jobs by being even more brutal than the SS guards.

A malnourished prisoner and his younger partner make strands of barbed-wire fencing, a relatively desirable assignment at Dachau.

Under close guard, a straining team of prisoners plows a field for planting. Each camp was required to produce its own food, which was always in short supply.

In the tailor shop at Sachsenhausen, prisoners with shaved heads sew striped, pajama-like uniforms for themselves and fellow inmates. From such shops grew the prison industry that provided the SS with its uniforms.

Freedom in Different Forms

Confinement in a concentration camp during the years 1933 to 1939 was not always a dead end. Some inmates were released after only a few weeks or months, and Hitler occasionally issued broad amnesties. In the first year alone, about 6,000 prisoners were let go.

For many internees, however, the only release was death. The SS guards had orders to shoot any prisoner who attempted to escape, refused to obey an order, or "indulged in any form of mutiny"—which amounted to an invitation to murder prisoners they disliked. "Any pity whatsoever for enemies of the state," the guards were taught, "is unworthy of an SS man."

In a photograph distributed by the government, a prisoner being released from Dachau under a 1933 amnesty shakes hands with his SS jailer. Paroled inmates had to sign an affidavit saying they had been well treated while in custody.

A prisoner lies sprawled across Dachau's electrified fence in 1939, his death either a suicide or a failed bid for freedom.

The Spread of a Malignant System

"The silent, ubiquitous threat hanging over every German," as one contemporary grimly described the concentration-camp system, grew only slowly during the mid-1930s. Releases and deaths of prisoners roughly balanced arrests, keeping the camp population under 25,000.

The number jumped dramatically, however, after Hitler's takeover of Austria and Czechoslovakia: Reinhard Heydrich's Gestapo swept up as many as 75,000 undesirables in those countries. The onset of war in 1939 brought another huge influx of captives from Poland and, later, from other conquered nations.

Nor was the Reich itself spared. In the month of October 1941, the Gestapo arrested 15,160 German-speaking people, mostly citizens suspected of impeding, or grumbling about, the war effort. The prison population soared to 220,000, and overcrowding was so rampant that in some camps one-fifth of the inmates died every six months.

Even this degree of carnage would be eclipsed later when the SS embarked on the madness of the "final solution," turning its camps into extermination centers for millions of Europe's Jews.

About 2,500 prisoners, a fraction of Germany's concentration-camp population, form ranks in the yard at Sachsenhausen in 1941. Lettered on the barracks in the background is the camp slogan, which all inmates had to memorize. It urges "self-sacrifice and love for the fatherland."

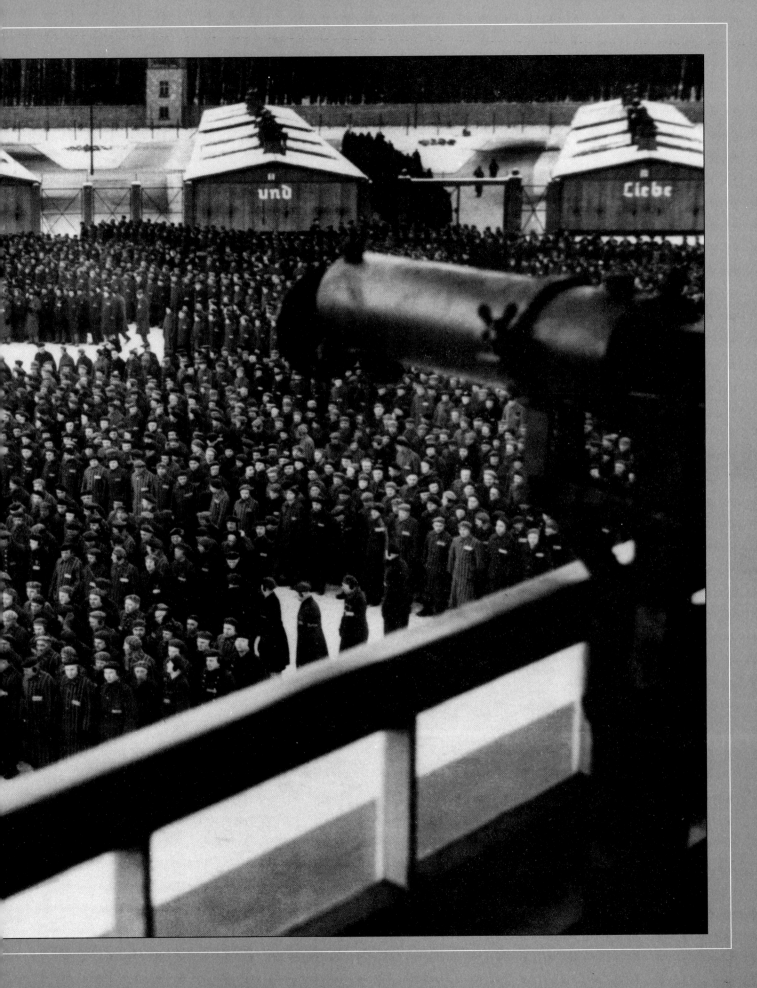

Uniforms to Set Off the Elite

Their uniforms were midnight black, broken only by silver braids and emblems, and the red, white, and black armbands of the Nazi party. At the rallies and official gatherings that were such important features of the Third Reich, members of Heinrich Himmler's SS never failed to stand out among the competing hosts of uniformed functionaries.

In 1930 the Reichsführer-SS, who was always preoccupied with the prestige and regalia of his men, abolished the old SA brown shirts and black ties that the Schutzstaffel had worn since 1925. The new black tunics, worn with breeches, knee-length riding boots, and Sam Browne belts, bore not only insignia of rank, but cuff bands that indicated the wearer's unit and specialty badges that designated his current duties and prior service in other organizations.

In 1934 the SS-VT, or special-purpose troops, began military training, and in the following year they were issued field uniforms in so-called earth gray, a warm gray-green color. By 1940, when the armed units became the Waffen-SS, they adopted army-style uniforms. The SS men retained their distinctive identity, however, by wearing the rank and unit markings from their peacetime dress. As the Waffen-SS expanded, new uniforms and insignia proliferated: SS tank crews adopted the army's black panzer jackets— fitting backgrounds for SS devices; newly created commands received unique cuff titles and badges; and camouflage smocks and helmet covers became trademarks of the Waffen-SS.

Despite worsening wartime shortages, most of the uniform requirements of Himmler's elite corps were met thanks to the output of concentration-camp industries run by the SS itself.

The first SS men wore outfits such as this one: a basic Storm Trooper uniform, with a black kepi, tie, breeches, and a black border on the armband. The skulls on their kepis were inspired by the field caps of the Imperial Life Guard Hussars in the nineteenth century.

The all-black tunic and peaked cap at left above were worn by a *Scharführer*, or staff sergeant, of the Allgemeine-SS Standarte 45, a regiment based at Oppeln in Upper Silesia. The red border on the cuff band indicates that the wearer belonged to the 3d Battalion. A braided aluminum chin strap marks the cap above as an officer's hat. The dress boots were worn by all ranks.

After 1935 members of SS-VT regiments wore earth gray cotton or wool-rayon uniforms for most duties. Their caps could be black or field gray, such as the one above. The tunic at right, issued to a *Sturmscharführer*, or sergeant major, was worn with belt and dagger as semiformal, or "walking-out" dress.

The white piping on the shoulder straps of the Waffen-SS tunic at right identifies the *Rottenführer*, or acting corporal, who wore it as a member of the infantry. The steel helmet, bearing the S-rune decal of the SS, replaced Germany's World War I-style helmet in 1936.

In 1940 the Waffen-SS adopted the army's black panzer jacket for its tank and armored-vehicle crews, and in 1941 substituted the black field caps *(far left)* for the ineffective, beret-style crash helmet *(left)*. In September of that year, a version of the jacket in field gray was ordered for the crews of assault guns and self-propelled antitank vehicles. The same jacket, made of rush green linen, was issued for fatigue wear.

The wool and rayon great coat above was common cold-weather gear for Waffen-SS men, as were the army-issue hobnailed boots. In 1943 the visored field cap, formerly worn only by mountain troops, became standard for all branches of the Waffen-SS.

The first *Tarnjacken*, or camouflage smocks *(left)*, were tested by the SS-VT regiment Deutschland in 1937. The prototype, augmented by a clip-on reversible helmet cover, was approved by Himmler in June 1938. Two years later camouflage clothing became general issue in the Waffen-SS.

This field cap, tunic, and parka are examples of the surprising variety of camouflage clothing developed by the SS during the war. Inconsistent oversight and a constant effort to improve concealment led to the proliferation of patterns. Among the camouflage garments were paratroop smocks, tank-crew coveralls, and panzer jackets.

Tropical tunics, made of lightweight cotton from an Italian pattern, and matching field caps were issued to SS troops for hot-weather wear in Italy, the Balkans, and southern Russia. As the war progressed, the combat shoes and short leggings (*above*) replaced the expensive jackboots.

After the first terrible winter of the Russian campaign, SS planners authorized production of cold-weather garments such as this parka and hat, both lined with fur, which were issued to panzer grenadiers in 1943.

THREE

Schemes of Subversion and Conquest

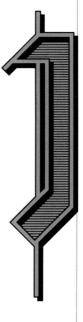

n the fall of 1933 Heinrich Himmler made his first foray into foreign affairs. His target was Austria, the country the Nazis coveted above all others for incorporation into their prospective Greater Germany. Annexation of his native land, Adolf Hitler had written in the first paragraph of *Mein Kampf,* was a "task to be furthered with every means our lives long."

Many Austrians shared Hitler's enthusiasm for *Anschluss,* or union. Membership in the Nazi party in Vienna alone had grown from 300 to some 40,000 in only three years. Nazi activities there, including sporadic incidents of sabotage, were encouraged by not only the party in Germany but no fewer than five different agencies of the German government, which were engaged in a bureaucratic battle for control of Reich policy in Austria.

Anschluss, however, had opponents in Austria, chief among them the country's chancellor, Engelbert Dollfuss. Though a diminutive man shorter than five feet tall, Dollfuss ran an iron-fisted regime modeled after that of his friend Benito Mussolini in Italy. There was no room in Dollfuss's program for extremist factions, and beginning in the summer of 1933, the chancellor cracked down on his opponents at both ends of the political spectrum, outlawing first the Nazi party and later the Socialist party.

Dollfuss's ban of the Nazis in his country inadvertently opened a door for Himmler and the SS. As thousands of Austrian Nazis fled across the border into Bavaria, Himmler was waiting to receive them. With Hitler's approval, the SS armed the émigrés and organized them into the Austrian Legion. This army in exile trained at a camp near the border, ready to return home when opportunity called. At the same time, Himmler's minions secretly signed up hundreds of SS members within Austria. Supplied with arms and explosives, the recruits energetically pursued a campaign of sabotage and terror, blowing up power stations and murdering supporters of the Dollfuss regime. By the beginning of 1934, the SS could count on 5,000 clandestine members in Austria. But they were a restless bunch, not always willing to follow the lead of their nominal German superiors.

One of the most ambitious and headstrong of the recruits was Fridolin Glass, a former sergeant major who had been drummed out of the Austrian

Officers of an SS *Einsatzgruppe,* or task force, that followed the German army into Poland in 1939 search Jews in Warsaw. The objective of the task forces, Himmler wrote, was to reduce the Polish population through terror to an abject, "leaderless labor force" for Germany.

army for activities in the Nazi SA—including the creation of his own little Brownshirt army of six companies. After his expulsion, Glass visited Himmler in Berlin and offered the services of his private army to the SS. Himmler approved, and the troops were incorporated into the SS as Standarte 89. Glass had more than sabotage in mind; he was plotting the overthrow of the Austrian regime. He intended to capture Dollfuss and his ministerial council, seize the main Vienna radio station, and proclaim a Nazi government. Himmler, carried along by the Austrian's enthusiasm, gave his approval for the coup attempt. Hitler evidently was informed, but the Führer cagily remained aloof from the details so that he could claim ignorance later if such dissembling proved expedient.

Glass's putsch, code-named Operation Summer Festival, took place on July 25, 1934. Shortly before one in the afternoon, Austrian army trucks carrying 150 troopers of the SS Standarte 89, some wearing army uniforms and others disguised as police, rolled up to the Federal Chancellery on Vienna's Ballhausplatz. Members of the assault party overwhelmed the guards, took the building, and stormed upstairs to where Chancellor Dollfuss was supposed to be meeting with his ministers. Dollfuss was there, but his cabinet was not. He had learned of the impending attack scarcely an hour earlier—a Nazi conspirator had betrayed the plotters at the last minute—and sent all but two of his colleagues to their offices.

When a contingent of ten SS men encountered Dollfuss, one of them fired at close range, hitting the chancellor in the neck and mortally wounding him. The putschists laid Dollfuss on a sofa and, while he slowly bled to death, harangued him with insults and political bombast, denying his requests for a doctor and a priest. Elsewhere in the city, fellow Nazis who had seized the radio station were broadcasting news that Dollfuss had resigned. But the putsch faltered as hundreds of other armed men in Vienna backed out on their pledge to join the revolt. These Austrians were SA members who evidently still resented the role played by the SS in the Blood Purge of Ernst Röhm and the SA leadership in Germany less than a month earlier. They looked on unmoved as government troops and police surrounded the chancellery and put an end to the putsch.

Hitler received word of Dollfuss's assassination that evening while attending a performance of *Das Rheingold* at the Wagner festival in Bayreuth. According to a witness, "The Führer could scarcely wipe the delight from his face." But the smirk disappeared when Hitler learned of Mussolini's reaction to the killing. At the time of the murder, Dollfuss's wife and two children happened to be houseguests of Mussolini in Italy, and the duce had to inform the wife of the assassination. Furious at this personal affront and at the threat to his neighbor's independence, Mussolini ordered 50,000

Flaunting Nazi armbands, young Austrian SS members convene at a hostelry in Innsbruck. Although the Nazi party was outlawed in Austria in 1933, hundreds of men continued to join the SS there and agitate against the government.

troops to the Brenner Pass on the Austrian border in a show of strength.

Hitler, realizing that his new Reich was not yet strong enough to bring about Anschluss by force of arms, disowned the Austrian affair that very day. At midnight the official German news agency withdrew the story prepared in celebration of Dollfuss's downfall and substituted a new version expressing regret at his "cruel murder."

The debacle embarrassed but did not deter Himmler. The Reichsführer-SS was supremely resilient. Driven by his hunger for power, he kept reaching for new realms of authority beyond the SS mandates to protect Hitler and maintain state security. In the years following the failure in Austria, Himmler involved the SS in a raft of schemes, from enforcing racial policy to exploiting slave labor as the Reich expanded eastward.

In time Austrian SS members atoned for the Dollfuss debacle. Held under much tighter control by Himmler and Hitler, they set up an intelligence network that kept the Reich informed of Austrian government affairs. SS operatives engineered the Nazi takeover of a powerful opposition movement that worked to undermine the Austrian regime. The SS also assisted in gaining the appointment of a pro-Nazi to the Austrian cabinet. The resulting political unrest set the stage for another attempt at Anschluss, and on March 12, 1938, Hitler sent his troops into Austria, securing the country with ease. It was a resounding triumph for nazism. Anschluss won

for the Reich an additional 6.5 million German-speaking people, encouraging the dreams of Hitler and Himmler for a racially pure Europe.

Himmler's obsession with racial purity motivated many of his schemes. At his behest, the SS kept a genealogical register of its members, and Himmler often pored over it like a horse breeder studying a studbook. Perhaps because his own appearance differed so markedly from the blond, blue-eyed Nordic stereotype, he ordered elaborate studies of his ancestry and that of his wife—presumably to gather irrefutable evidence of their pure German lineage.

The SS chief was concerned as well with the racial ancestry of the entire German people. In 1935 he founded the Ancestral Heritage Society, whose role was to study the origins of his fellow Germans. Financed by a group of wealthy industrialists, the institute sponsored such Himmler-inspired schemes as an expedition to Tibet to research the history of the Asian peoples who had migrated to Europe about fifteen centuries earlier. The organization also began excavations in East Prussia and Bavaria to unearth thousand-year-old ruins from the time of Himmler's medieval hero, Henry the Fowler, a Saxon duke who founded the German state and became King Heinrich I in the year 919. Heinrich had expanded his realm by pushing eastward at the expense of the Slavs; Himmler, too, believed that he was destined to colonize those old Germanic lands now ruled by the Slavs of Czechoslovakia, Poland, and the Soviet Union.

While the Ancestral Heritage Society indulged Himmler's hobby, his main instrument for racial matters was the Race and Settlement Central Office, known by its German acronym, RUSHA. Established in 1931 with Himmler's mentor Walther Darré as director, RUSHA had started as a standards bureau to insure that SS recruits and their prospective brides measured up genetically. Himmler envisioned his SS as a biological elite—the "grandsires," as he put it, of the new Germany. Spurred by this vision, RUSHA planners created the position of *Rassenprüfer*, or race examiner—white-coated technicians with calipers and measuring tapes who lent a veneer of science to the nonsense concocted by Darré and Himmler.

RUSHA soon pushed its tentacles into other realms of influence. After Darré gained the additional post of food and agriculture minister, RUSHA performed research on rural-settlement techniques. Himmler, the former chicken farmer, and Darré, the ideologue, fantasized about a new feudal

Assigned by Himmler to develop techniques for racial selection, SS official Walther Darré, shown above, dreamed up pseudo-scientific tests of the ideal Aryan physiognomy, a look epitomized at right in sketches made by Nazi artists. The tests, photographed in 1937 (*above, right*), included matching hair colors and swatches of tinted fiberglass, and measuring the dimensions of a subject's face and cranium. Such procedures were used by SS racial examiners to select individuals of acceptable stock.

Europe consisting of model farms operated by a racial elite. They encouraged SS men to take up farming in pursuit of the blood-and-soil mystique.

At Himmler's instigation, RUSHA also established a network of family-welfare offices to care for widows and orphans of SS members. This project reflected Himmler's concern with Germany's lagging birthrate. World War I had decimated the German male population, and economic hardship during the Great Depression had discouraged marriage. As a result, the nation by 1935 was producing babies at only about half the rate of fifty years earlier. Himmler campaigned against anything that might hold down the birthrate —contraception, abortion, even the possession of pets when they served as psychological substitutes for children.

Above all, he encouraged procreation. He announced that it was the patriotic duty of every man in the SS to sire at least four children. (Himmler himself fell one child short: He had a daughter by his wife Margarete and a son and a daughter by the secretary he later took as his mistress.) In 1939 he flatly ordered all SS men to impregnate their wives and, when possible, to serve as "conception assistants" to childless women aged thirty or older.

Out of Himmler's campaign to foster procreation grew one of the most remarkable of the myriad SS agencies. In December 1935 the Reichsführer ordered RUSHA to establish the Lebensborn, or Fountain of Life, a network of maternity homes "to accommodate and look after racially and genetically valuable expectant mothers"—the wives and girlfriends of SS men. The first Lebensborn home began operation in 1936 near Munich; eventually, scores more were opened in Germany and occupied countries.

Mothers could keep the children born at the homes or place them for adoption with SS-approved families. Involuntary deductions from the wages of SS officers helped support the Lebensborn, although increasingly it was financed by expropriation of the bank accounts and property of Jews.

Not all Germans viewed Lebensborn with the reverence that Himmler might have wished. The homes often were derided as brothels or "human stud farms." But Himmler was undeterred by criticism. He placed the project under his own supervision and took an intense interest in its procedures. Every detail fascinated him, from the shapes of the noses of mothers and children to the volume of milk produced by nursing mothers, the most prolific of whom received special recognition. He served as nominal godfather to thousands of children born in the homes, and those who entered the world on his birthday, October 7, received toys and other gifts. His eyes filled with tears when a Lebensborn child died, but he refused to hear reports of children with mental or physical handicaps. Such human abnormalities did not accord with his dream of a super race of SS offspring.

In addition to founding racially oriented agencies, the SS also won control of another such organization with an even wider franchise. Known as VOMI, for *Volksdeutsche Mittelstelle*, the Liaison Office for Ethnic Germans dealt with the large group of Germanics abroad that Himmler and other Nazis considered crucial to their vision of an enlarged Reich. VOMI eventually uprooted and moved as many as 1.2 million ethnic Germans.

Most of these Volksdeutsche lived in central and eastern Europe. Beginning in the Middle Ages, their ancestors had moved eastward from the original German territory to find new land and livelihoods. Settling in an enormous region stretching from the Baltic provinces to the Volga and the Caucasus, the migrants formed closely knit communities that remained aloof from their neighbors and retained strong ties of kinship with the old homeland. The Nazis were counting on the ethnic Germans to augment the Reich's depleted population and to help in the expansion eastward. "I really intend to take German blood from wherever it is to be found in the world," Himmler vowed, "to rob and steal it wherever I can."

The nascent VOMI—it was not named that at first—had been established in 1936 as a secret agency within the party. Hitler wanted it to coordinate relations with the ethnic Germans, remedying the confusion caused by too many groups—from the Foreign Ministry to the private Association for Germanism Abroad—competing for power in foreign communities. The 1934 debacle in Austria had demonstrated the dangers of such internecine intrigues. But VOMI's influence was slow to develop. It seemed incapable of exercising the control needed to facilitate Hitler's expansion plans.

Himmler, seeing his chance to gain a foothold for the SS in foreign policy,

This 1940 poster, showing a German woman nursing her infant, was used to solicit contributions for the Nazi organization Mutter und Kind (Mother and Child), which sought to spur Germany's lagging birthrate by providing maternity services for working and unwed mothers. The SS cared for the mates of its men at its Lebensborn homes.

arranged for the appointment of one of his own men as the director of VOMI. His choice was Werner Lorenz, an SS lieutenant general and the SS chief in the Hamburg area. A handsome World War I pilot, Lorenz had a large estate near Danzig and the sophistication to go with it. He was a Prussian nationalist who knew little about the problems of the Germans abroad, and proved to be patronizing in his attitude toward Himmler's racial ideas. Himmler tolerated these shortcomings because Lorenz was the perfect frontman, a skillful diplomat who could move adroitly from the drawing room to the country markets, where he liked to talk crops with the farmers.

Under Lorenz the Liaison Office performed so efficiently that in July 1938 Hitler increased its power. VOMI absorbed other agencies, brought together rival factions in the ethnic German communities, and funneled in money to build clubrooms and hospitals and to spread Nazi propaganda. VOMI also investigated the politics of individual ethnic Germans and began compiling files on people suspected of disloyalty to the Führer.

Although VOMI was not formally incorporated into the SS until 1941, Himmler quickly made it his own creature. He infiltrated SS men into it and persuaded its staff to join the SS. Himmler's men appeared in leadership positions in cultural organizations such as the German Bulgarian Society. He installed as Lorenz's deputy an SS colleague, Hermann Behrends, a hard-nosed veteran of Reinhard Heydrich's SD. Originally a party agency for gathering domestic intelligence, the SD was evolving into an instrument for espionage abroad. Heydrich and Behrends used VOMI to place SD agents in the far-flung communities of ethnic Germans in eastern Europe.

Control of VOMI failed to sate Himmler's appetite for power; he hungered for influence in the most important agency concerned with affairs in the East—the Foreign Ministry. His opportunity came in February 1938, when Hitler appointed Himmler's friend Joachim von Ribbentrop as foreign minister. A former ambassador to Britain who had married the heir to the Henkell champagne fortune, Ribbentrop first encountered Himmler upon joining the party in 1932. Himmler was attracted by the glamorous social circle in which Ribbentrop moved and cultivated the newcomer, making him a colonel in the SS and soon promoting him to general. Ribbentrop,

Himmler *(left)* and a somber-looking Werner Lorenz—chosen by Himmler to head the powerful Liaison Office for Ethnic Germans—confer in 1939 at a ceremony conducted to welcome ethnic Germans from the Ukraine back to the Reich. Their return was part of an agreement with Josef Stalin.

a man of more vanity than ability, reciprocated by appointing SS men to his staff when he served the Führer in various foreign-policy advisory posts.

Soon after his appointment as foreign minister, Ribbentrop asked his old friend to accept into the SS as a body all the ministry's senior bureaucrats. Himmler was happy to oblige. Ribbentrop even good-naturedly chided Himmler for not making enough of his black-suited minions available for duty in the ministry. An aide said later that nothing gave Ribbentrop greater pleasure than "to appear in the office in the uniform of an SS Gruppen-führer with his great jackboots." The day would come, however, when struggles for power within the bureaucracy would turn Himmler and Ribbentrop into enemies; then the foreign minister would fly into a rage if he saw one of his diplomats wearing the formerly prized black uniform.

Himmler first exercised the new authority of the SS in foreign affairs in next-door Czechoslovakia. A polyglot nation created when the old Austro-Hungarian Empire was carved up after World War I, Czechoslovakia was home to more than three million people of German descent. Most of these ethnic Germans lived in the country's western part, known as the Sude-tenland, for the Sudetic Mountains. The presence of these people became the wedge by which Hitler began to splinter the Czech republic in 1938.

VOMI was an agency the SS used to penetrate Sudeten communities. Agents of the Liaison Office played upon the grievances of the Sudeten Germans, who had been hard hit by the depression and felt mistreated by the central government. SS funds subsidized the Sudeten German party,

the political organization that claimed the allegiance of nearly all the ethnic Germans, and VOMI officials met regularly with the party's leaders.

The other major SS instrument in the Sudetenland, the SD, operated more covertly. The SD had been involved with Sudeten refugees in Germany as early as 1933, and Heydrich developed a network of agents across the border, planting them in clubs, cultural groups, universities, and within the Sudeten German party itself. These agents generated so much information, wrote Heydrich's deputy Walter Schellenberg, "that in order to handle all the incoming messages, special telegraph lines running direct to Berlin had to be installed at two points on the German-Czech frontier."

The leader of the Sudeten German party, Konrad Henlein, a mild-mannered former bank clerk and gymnastics teacher, received special attention from Heydrich, whose SD devoted a small department just to monitoring his activities. Heydrich and Himmler both distrusted Henlein because he was a relative moderate, a nationalist who failed to demonstrate sufficient enthusiasm for the Reich and its Führer and advocated political and cultural autonomy for his people. As late as 1937 he still hoped to achieve that goal peacefully through parliamentary action in the Czech government—and to avoid being gobbled up in a German invasion.

Heydrich did his best to depose Henlein. Repeatedly, he wrote memorandums to Hitler trying to discredit the Sudeten leader. Among other charges, he suggested that Henlein, who had visited London seeking support for self-determination, was no more than a lackey of the British secret service. Heydrich also cultivated Nazis within the radical wing of the Sudeten German party who supported incorporation of the Sudetenland into the Reich. He won the allegiance of Henlein's deputy, Carl Hermann Frank, and through him attempted to foment revolt within the party. Although the SS failed to bring down Henlein, its machinations isolated the Sudeten leader and helped drive him into Hitler's arms. So, too, did Germany's annexation of neighboring Austria in March 1938. The ease of the Anschluss forced Henlein's hand by rousing enormous enthusiasm among his own people and by convincing Hitler that the Sudetenland— indeed all of Czechoslovakia—was also ripe for plucking. Henlein met two times with the Führer and caved in to the inevitable.

By the summer of 1938 Henlein was in line. With Hitler's approval, a paramilitary force, the Freikorps Henlein, was organized to "maintain disorders and clashes" in the Sudetenland, and the SS-dominated VOMI helped form a secret fifth column to subvert the Czech government in the event of a German invasion. As it happened, the mere threat of invasion sufficed. The Czech government ceded the Sudetenland to Germany as of October 1, 1938. Henlein's reward was a relatively unimportant post as

Sudeten Germans effusively salute Hitler in late 1938, after Czechoslovakia ceded the border area to Germany.

Fleeing the Sudetenland after the German takeover, loyal Czechs wait to entrain for other parts of the country.

gauleiter, or Nazi leader, in the Sudetenland—and the rank of SS general, conferred upon him by the men who had undermined him and helped thwart his people's independence.

The emergence of the SS as a force in foreign policy had relegated Ribbentrop's diplomats to a back seat during the Sudeten crisis. The German minister in Prague, who opposed annexation, was kept in the dark at the height of the affair. Then, with the Sudetenland absorbed into the Reich, Hitler bypassed his Foreign Ministry and looked to the SD as he plotted the takeover of the rest of Czechoslovakia.

Following Hitler's seizure of the remainder of Czechoslovakia in March 1939, a Nazi functionary ringed by SS men and customs officials removes the Czech national emblem from a boundary post at the frontier of the Sudetenland.

Late in January 1939 Hitler assigned Heydrich and other leading members of the SD key roles in the final dismemberment of Czechoslovakia. The Führer's plan hinged upon provoking trouble in the eastern province of Slovakia. Feelings of nationalism there had been stirred by similar fervor in the Sudeten Germans, and although the Czech government had recently granted semi-autonomy to the Slovaks, a campaign for complete independence was gaining momentum. Hitler wanted agents from the SD to stoke those fires and ignite political chaos. This would give the Führer a pretext for acting as the benevolent protector of all Czechoslovakia.

Under Hitler's orders, the SD proceeded in secrecy. A team of agents led by SS General Wilhelm Keppler traveled to the Slovakian provincial capital of Bratislava. They met there with leaders of the dominant Slovak Peoples' party, an ultranationalist and conservative group that numbered many Roman Catholic priests in its top rank. Keppler and his men enjoyed a warm reception—"We found the Slovaks eager to fall in with our plans," wrote one of the agents, Wilhelm Hoettl. But a key figure, Slovak Minister of State Karel Sidor, balked, and the negotiations stalled.

To hurry matters along, Heydrich decided to demonstrate to the doubting Sidor—and the Czechs—how much the Slovaks wanted independence. He dispatched to Slovakia another kind of SD team, a sabotage squad commanded by Alfred Naujocks, a former mechanic and now an SS major. Naujocks was Heydrich's troubleshooter, in charge of forging passports, blowing up buildings, and causing incidents to appear to be the work of

someone else. In Bratislava, Naujocks's men set off bombs in a chocolate factory and made it seem that Slovak nationalists were to blame. The Czech government responded as the Germans anticipated; Prague dismissed the Slovak government and declared a state of emergency in Slovakia.

By March 12 the SS effort to finish off Czechoslovakia had reached a crescendo. In Prague, VOMI organized street demonstrations; SS terrorist teams arrived in Slovakia and the province of Bohemia to carry out further acts of provocation; in Bratislava, Keppler was again negotiating with Slovak politicians. Early the next day, Josef Tiso, the portly priest whom the Czechs had recently deposed as prime minister, gave in to the pressure from the SD. He announced his willingness to proclaim the sovereignty of Slovakia under German protection. The following day Tiso took the train to Vienna, then flew in a special SD aircraft to Berlin to inform the Führer. Within a few days German troops would occupy Slovakia. And on March 15, rather than risk war, the president of Czechoslovakia agreed to German "protection" of the provinces of Bohemia and Moravia, while Hungary grabbed the easternmost and last remaining province, Ruthenia.

That day, when Hitler's motorcade triumphantly entered Prague, the Führer was accompanied by two top foreign-policy aides. One was Foreign Minister Ribbentrop, the other Himmler. Despite blatant signs of SS incursion into his jurisdiction, Ribbentrop had failed to learn his lesson. A few months later, and much to his subsequent regret, Ribbentrop agreed to the placement of SD agents in German embassies and legations to provide cover for their spying and other endeavors. The SD intelligence chief in a country was accorded diplomatic status and given the title police attaché. In exchange, the SD promised not to interfere in matters of policy. Soon, however, these attachés were filing reports critical of German diplomats—not to Ribbentrop, but directly to Heydrich and Himmler.

The maneuverings in Austria and Czechoslovakia served as rehearsals for the SS. The invasion of Poland on September 1, 1939, which marked the beginning of World War II, tested in earnest the increasing capabilities of Himmler's organization. Here, in a land that Hitler intended not merely to occupy but to destroy, Himmler's men were cast in many guises—as provocateurs, police, killers, and managers of forced movements of people.

The SS role began in late August 1939, shortly before the Wehrmacht invaded Poland. To avoid international opprobrium, Hitler needed an excuse for the invasion, and he looked to the SS to provide it. Heydrich dreamed up scores of incidents that could be attributed to Polish extremists and thus justify a German attack. These charades were to be played out by a dozen teams of his SD and police agents acting under the overall

Reinhard Heydrich *(left)*, appointed "protector" of Czechoslovakia in 1941, mounts the steps of his grand Prague headquarters with his smiling SS subordinate Carl Hermann Frank, a prominent Sudeten German who had abetted Heydrich's schemes during the takeover of the country.

command of the Gestapo chief Heinrich Müller. Several of the incidents called for SD agents dressed in Polish army uniforms to fake attacks on the German border. To make the raids more realistic, the script dictated that some of the assailants die in action so their bodies could be offered later as proof of Polish aggression. The deaths indeed occurred, but the casualties were in fact prisoners from a German concentration camp who had been given fatal injections just before the attack, then riddled with bullets. The Gestapo cynically referred to the victims as "canned goods."

The most important of the bogus raids was launched against a German radio station at the border town of Gleiwitz on August 31. Alfred Naujocks, the Heydrich troubleshooter whose expertise with explosives had helped hasten the crisis in Slovakia earlier that year, took over the station at gunpoint with five accomplices. One of them, speaking Polish, broadcast an inflammatory diatribe, declaring that Poland was invading Germany. The provocateurs fired a few shots for the benefit of the radio audience and then fled, leaving behind one of the dead concentration-camp inmates. On the following day, Hitler, citing the attack at Gleiwitz, announced that the Wehrmacht had invaded Poland at dawn. The "canned goods" left at the

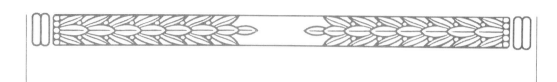

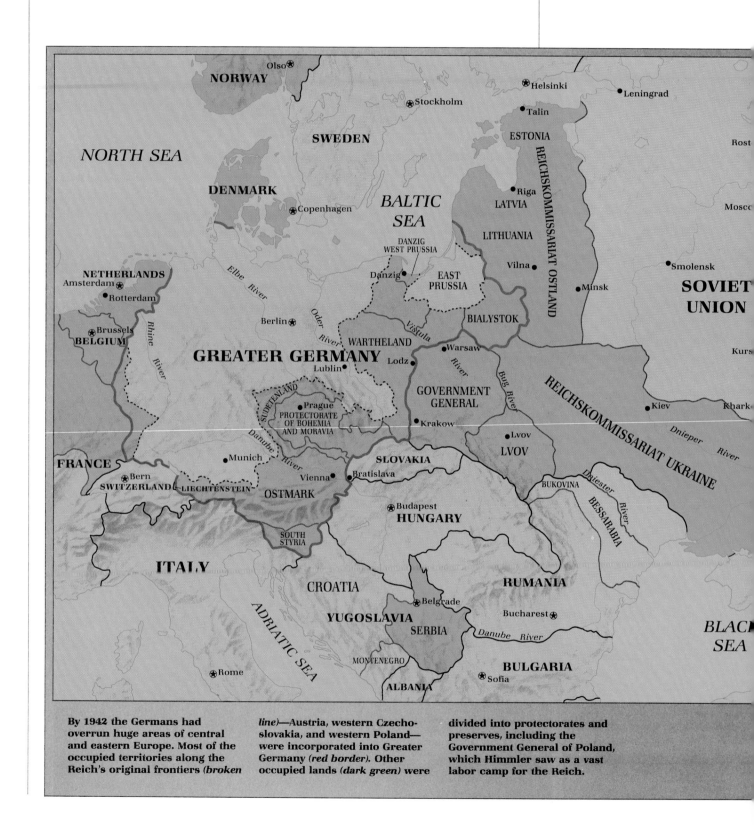

By 1942 the Germans had overrun huge areas of central and eastern Europe. Most of the occupied territories along the Reich's original frontiers (*broken line*)—Austria, western Czechoslovakia, and western Poland—were incorporated into Greater Germany (*red border*). Other occupied lands (*dark green*) were divided into protectorates and preserves, including the Government General of Poland, which Himmler saw as a vast labor camp for the Reich.

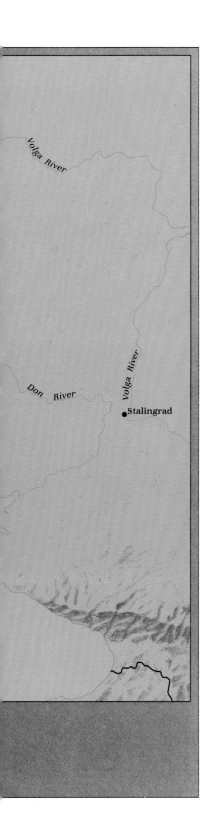

radio station were exhibited to the press as proof of the provocation.

As the German army swept through Poland, the SS followed, energetically performing its next role in the destruction of that nation: the liquidation of the political and cultural elite. Hitler knew this was no task for regular soldiers. At a meeting of his Wehrmacht commanders less than a fortnight before the invasion, he had warned that "things would be done of which German generals would not approve," as Field Marshal Fedor von Bock recalled. "He did not therefore wish to burden the army with the necessary liquidations, but would have them carried out by the SS."

Himmler entrusted this mission of mass killing to mobile SD and Security Police detachments that bore the innocuous name *Einsatzgruppen*, or task forces. They had seen limited and less grisly action during the annexation of Austria and the breakup of Czechoslovakia. For the Polish campaign, one Einsatzgruppe of 400 to 600 men was assigned to each of the five invading armies; a sixth unit was deployed in the border province of Poznan, a former Prussian territory that Hitler intended to reclaim for the Reich.

To oversee the Einsatzgruppen in Poland, another new government agency, the Reich Central Security Office, or RSHA, was created and placed under Heydrich's control. RSHA brought together the Gestapo, Criminal Police, and SD; thus were concentrated in one office, as an observer of the Reich put it, "all the powers of spying and intelligence, interrogation and arrest, torture and execution on which dictatorship ultimately depends."

The Einsatzgruppen worked methodically from previously prepared lists of names. Aristocrats, priests, government officials, business people, teachers, and physicians—all were rounded up and herded into hastily improvised reception camps behind the advancing Wehrmacht. Execution by shooting usually took place there soon afterward. In one Roman Catholic diocese, two-thirds of the 690 priests were arrested; 214 were executed. Among the arrested were many Jews, and they too became victims. Although no general instructions singling out Jews for execution had yet been handed down, at least one Einsatzgruppe leader, SS General Udo von Woyrsch, took it upon himself to concentrate on killing Jewish people.

Local political leaders also were prime targets for murder. Jakub Krugieski, mayor of the city of Poznan, and his wife Magdalena lived on an estate outside the city, and after the German takeover the mayor and his family remained at home in seclusion. For a time it seemed that they would be spared. Although they heard shots in the distance every day, their privacy was unbroken. Then one day the SS arrived. The mayor's daughter Lucy, who was eighteen, would never forget what happened. She had gone to feed her horse, a two-year-old Arabian that her father had given her. "As I returned from the stable, I saw in the rear garden about fifty men in

uniforms, some wearing helmets, others in soft caps, many carrying machine guns. They had their backs to me." Facing the men, against the wall of their house, stood her parents. Lucy's father caught sight of her and shouted, "Run!" With that the men fired, and she saw her parents fall.

Lucy fled through some woods, hid for three days in a potato field, and then was taken in by an employee of the estate. Eventually, she ventured into the city, was arrested and deported in a cattle car to Hamburg, where she was pressed into service as a maid. Her parents were buried with other victims of the SS in a mass grave near Poznan.

The "SS reign of terror in Poland," as a German diplomat described it in his diary, progressed efficiently. By September 8, a week after the invasion, SS commanders were boasting of a death toll of 200 Poles a day. On

SS executioners lead their blindfolded Polish victims one by one into the Palmiry Forest, where thousands of Warsaw's citizens were put to death.

A firing squad of task-force commandos adds to the pile of corpses in a clearing near the Polish town of Bydgoszcz, where SS Major Manfred Roeder carried out Hitler's dictum that "whatever we find in the shape of an upper class in Poland will be liquidated."

September 27 Heydrich announced, "Of the Polish upper classes in the occupied territories only a maximum of three percent is still present."

Soon members of the Einsatzgruppen began operating alongside death squads of another variety, the so-called self-defense units. They consisted of ethnic Germans who had been objects of a brief Polish hate campaign waged in the days after the invasion. Mobs had sacked German houses and farms, and perhaps 5,000 Germans were murdered; some 50,000 were forced from their homes in western Poland. Unlike the Reich's task groups, which worked in a rational, cold-blooded manner, the self-defense units were driven by a lust for revenge. As soon as the Wehrmacht had rolled past, men from the German minority banded together in volunteer militias that soon degenerated into marauding bands bent upon killing Poles. Anti-Polish feeling was pronounced in West Prussia, where the gauleiter of Danzig, Albert Forster, moved in to spread hatred's flames.

Himmler was not pleased by this turn of events. When he saw Forster, an old foe, gaining influence, Himmler moved to protect what he regarded as his preserve. He sent the chief of his recruiting office, Lieutenant General Gottlob Berger, to take charge of the self-defense units and bring them under SS control. Berger divided the units into four groups and assigned a German SS commander to each. Although the units were to serve as auxiliary police forces, some continued on rampages so murderous that even Heydrich showed concern. Evidently worried more about the lack of discipline than the lack of humanity in these newly inducted SS men, he complained of "certain intolerable and uncontrolled acts of revenge."

Even before the self-defense units had joined in the killing, many German

soldiers had begun questioning the activities of the Einsatzgruppen. Although in the operations zone the task groups were technically under army command, Hitler had ordered that their heinous mission be kept secret from the regular forces and camouflaged by such euphemisms as "counterespionage work." But the soldiers realized the truth, and many were appalled; as Heydrich noted dryly, "to the uninitiated the action of the police and SS appeared arbitrary, brutal, and unauthorized." On September 20 the operations section of the Fourteenth Army reported, "The troops are especially incensed that, instead of fighting at the front, young men should be demonstrating their courage against defenseless civilians."

More than one senior Wehrmacht officer was also worried. Admiral Wilhelm Canaris, chief of the *Abwehr*, or military intelligence, told the high command that "the world will one day hold the Wehrmacht responsible for these methods since these things are taking place under its nose." Pressure from the army forced the SS to suspend temporarily the operations of the most vicious task group, that of Udo von Woyrsch in southern Poland. But most generals were willing to look the other way, content to leave the dirty work to the SS.

In mid-October, about three weeks after the fighting in Poland had ended, Hitler relieved the Wehrmacht of principal responsibility for the occupation. He established a crazy-quilt system of rule that incorporated some areas into existing political regions of the Reich and set up others as new parts of Germany. He lumped the remainder of the country—except for the eastern portion, which the Soviet Union had overrun—into a colony called the Government General of Poland. Hitler's generals were aghast at the burgeoning bureaucratic nightmare. So eager were they to end their occupation duties and stay clear of this maze of competing authorities that they pulled out before the new administrations were solidly in place.

Into the vacuum stepped Himmler, to take over all police matters and to rule a shadow regime in the Government General. The Einsatzgruppen settled in to police the occupation. Meanwhile, the campaign against the Polish elite continued apace—now without complaints from the generals. In the spring of 1940, more than six months after the killing started, the Einsatzgruppen executed an additional 3,500 Poles.

Himmler, meanwhile, had embarked on another venture to further his dream of a racially pure Greater Germany. In October 1939 he became czar of a cruelly ambitious scheme for the resettlement of Poland that would affect the lives of more than a million Eastern Europeans and prompt a high-ranking SS racial specialist to exult, "The East belongs to the SS."

Like many of Himmler's projects, resettlement began with less grandiose

proportions. During September the advance of the Red Army into eastern Poland had brought some 136,000 ethnic Germans under Soviet occupation. In discussions with Berlin, the Russians agreed to let these people leave. In addition, the Reich negotiated for the transfer of another 120,000 Germans living in the Baltic states. Hitler asked VOMI, the Liaison Office for Ethnic Germans, to come up with a plan for resettlement of these people.

When Himmler heard of this, he immediately perceived a glowing opportunity. Newly conquered Poland would be the ideal place to resettle the ethnic Germans—perhaps even in the kind of feudal peasant aristocracy he and Walther Darré had dreamed of. To make room for them, the indigenous Slavs and Jews could be removed or reduced to serfdom. Himmler went to Hitler and persuaded the Führer to put him in charge of the entire project. He arranged to have Hitler issue a decree authorizing the scheme on October 7, 1939—Himmler's thirty-ninth birthday.

The growing versatility of the SS could be applied to the relocation plan. VOMI, dominated by the SS, was the most experienced agency in dealing with Germans abroad; it would transport the repatriates, care for them in reception camps, and supervise political indoctrination. RUSHA, the Race and Settlement Central Office, would handle matters of racial purity, though without the direction of Himmler's old mentor Darré, who had been forced to resign after Himmler found his ideological training of SS recruits "too theoretical." (Darré, who remained the food and agriculture minister, complained that Himmler had squeezed him "like a lemon"; Himmler relented later, allowing Darré to oversee the settlement of farmers in Poland.) The police and SD, under Heydrich's RSHA, would confiscate property and resettle what Hitler called "Jews, Poles, and similar trash."

To coordinate all of these existing agencies, however, Himmler felt compelled to set up a new one, which in the acronym-addicted SS was known as the RKFDV—from the German for Reich Commission for the Strengthening of Germanism. Himmler named as its chief Ulrich Greifelt, a Berliner who had managed a manufacturing plant before losing his job during the depression. He was an SS officer with a reputation as a technocrat—more at home with production statistics than with racial ideology. He had successfully managed an earlier resettlement problem: the repatriation of ethnic Germans from the South Tyrol just inside the Italian border.

Greifelt also had served as Himmler's liaison with the Four-Year Plan, Hermann Göring's enterprise aimed at stimulating German industry. This connection was a key to the selection of Greifelt to lead the RKFDV. Greifelt had suggested that Greater Germany's pressing labor shortage—estimated at 500,000 workers in January 1939—could be solved by repatriating ethnic Germans. Himmler had little choice but to listen. Fantasies about idyllic

agricultural settlements notwithstanding, Himmler was under orders to bring "home to the Reich" people to staff the factories and farms that had been depleted by army recruitment and the thriving armaments industry.

The cumbersome and cruel machinery of resettlement cranked into gear during that autumn of 1939. By the tens of thousands, people moved in two massive crosscurrents. Ethnic Germans from the Baltic states and Soviet-occupied Poland were uprooted and transported westward by ship and train to the newly annexed territories of the Reich. (Their number eventually doubled to 500,000 with the arrival of distant kin from Rumania, Yugoslavia, and other eastern countries wracked by war.) Even greater numbers of Slavs and Jews were pried loose from their farms and homes and deported eastward into the Government General of Poland.

From the beginning, Himmler and his resettlement bureaucracy encountered obstacles set up by competing Nazi power centers in the occupied lands. As in Germany itself, petty potentates abounded, each intent upon carving a niche of influence and riches in this vulnerable new empire. Albert Forster, the Nazi leader in Danzig and West Prussia, was so antagonistic to the prospect of taking settlers into his domain that ships carrying German repatriates from Estonia to Danzig had to be rerouted. Other gauleiters also refused to allow resettlement. Himmler, moreover, had to battle with representatives of Göring's Four-Year Plan for control of farms confiscated from Poles and Jews. The infighting among members of Himmler's own satrapy eventually took its toll. During a quarrel with Himmler, Ulrich Greifelt, the head of the resettlement-coordinating office, suffered a nervous breakdown and spent the next five months in a sanatarium.

The effect of this squabbling was to compound the hardships of the ethnic Germans. Many were forced to swap the comforts of home and farm for months of rootless existence in resettlement camps. Families were temporarily split, longtime homes lost, belongings misplaced. In the 1,500 camps maintained by VOMI, the repatriates underwent the seemingly perpetual process of proving their German heritage to black-clad SS officers, brown-shirted party officials, gray-uniformed bureaucrats, and white-coated examiners from the Race and Settlement Central Office. Moving through mazes of rooms and tables, the migrants had their papers scrutinized, their bodies photographed, x-rayed, and measured, and the color of their hair and eyes gawked at. Finally, each received a score, ranging from I-a-M/1 (racially very valuable) to IV-3-C (racial reject). From these marks and other factors, their futures were determined: resettlement in the East, employment in Germany, or if doubts existed about their loyalty or ethnic origin, a longer stay in camp and additional screening.

The German repatriates were in any event fortunate compared to the

An Ordeal in Limbo

The photographs below and on the following two pages, taken by an official German photographer, document conditions in a makeshift camp where Jews from Kutno, Poland, were confined for two years. Their ordeal began in September 1939, when SS men murdered many of Kutno's 6,700 Jews and plundered their neighborhood. Early in 1940 the survivors were interned on a debris-strewn lot outside town where many of them had to improvise crude shelters. During two harsh winters, typhoid and other diseases killed thousands of the inmates. Then, in March 1942, those who endured were herded into the extermination camp at Chelmno, where all perished.

Two young women of Kutno keep company by the prison-ghetto's barbed-wire fence.

Inmates fashion a hovel from a horse cart.

Combating the squalor, a woman does her wash.

A Kutno matron polishes a tattered boot as her children gather around an old sofa and other pieces of salvaged furniture.

Amid the trash-filled chaos of the Kutno camp, a junked car serves as home for a resourceful family.

A woman prepares a meal on an outdoor stove as her husband looks on.

people they replaced. An estimated 1.5 million Jews and other Poles were marked for removal from the western regions of Poland. The deportations began in earnest during the winter of 1939-1940, when temperatures sometimes plummeted to forty degrees below zero. Evacuees were packed into unheated trains that often were shuttled about needlessly on sidings. When the trains finally squealed to a halt in eastern Poland, they sometimes contained only frozen corpses. Himmler, addressing his SS field troops later in the war, boasted of the "toughness" required to carry out such an assignment. "In many cases it is much easier to go into battle with a company of infantry," said the Reichsführer-SS, "than it is to suppress an obstructive population of low cultural level, or to carry out executions, or to haul people away, or to evict crying and hysterical women."

During that terrible winter, about 87,000 Jews were hauled eastward to a region between two rivers, the Vistula and Bug, that divided the German and Soviet occupation zones. There, southwest of Lublin, land had been marked for resettlement. The relocation project was the work of an industrious SS officer named Adolf Eichmann, a former traveling salesman who was considered an expert on Jewish affairs, having earlier arranged the deportation of half the Austrian Jewish population. Eichmann's scheme in Poland, however, caught the governor general of Poland, Hans Frank, in the middle. He was expected to feed and absorb a stream of deportees flowing from the west; at the same time he was to fulfill the labor needs of Göring's Four-Year Plan by exporting more than one million Poles to the Old Reich. In February 1940 Frank appealed to Göring, who temporarily banned shipments to Eichmann's planned reservation. But by the middle of 1941, an estimated one million Poles and Jews had been resettled in Frank's domain, and some 200,000 ethnic Germans had claimed the vacant farms, homes, and businesses in the annexed territories.

This was not enough for Himmler. He wanted to repatriate not only people of established German ancestry, but even Poles whose blue eyes and blond hair suggested Nordic forebears. Vowing to Hitler that he would remove "every valuable trace of German blood from Poledom," Himmler sent his racial examiners in pursuit of Poles who might be concealing their ancestry. They were to be taken to the Old Reich and Germanized.

The motives for the Germanization program were pragmatic as well as ideological. The Reich needed laborers—male and female. Himmler took an interest in the recruiting and Germanizing of young Polish women aged sixteen to twenty who possessed the proper Nordic appearance. They were needed as household helpers for large German families—a project his bureaucrats appropriately dubbed Operation Nursemaid.

But Himmler recognized that the best candidates for Germanization

German soldiers, meeting Himmler's demand that "racially pure children of Poles" be absorbed by the Reich, wrench a blond girl from her mother. Of the 200,000 Polish children kidnapped and dispatched to Germany, only 20,000 could be located at the war's end.

were young children. His SS racial examiners searched orphanages and sometimes the streets of Poland for youngsters of mixed parentage, distant German ancestry, or simply Nordic appearance. The SS kidnapped suitable candidates and turned them over to its Lebensborn project, which soon opened homes in Poland. Lebensborn gave the children new names and found German SS couples of undoubted loyalty to raise them. In this way more than 200,000 Polish children became Germans during World War II.

Himmler was concerned too with the Germanization of another Polish resource, its industrial plants. He wanted to expand into occupied Poland the considerable economic empire already established by the SS. The agency's venture into the business world had started modestly enough in 1934 with the founding of a publishing house to popularize Himmler's racial ideas; two years later the SS purchased a porcelain factory to provide cultic knickknacks for the secret order. Soon, however, business became a way to help finance the SS and give it an increasing measure of independence from both the state and the party.

In 1938 Himmler started to tap the concentration camps under SS control as sources of labor. After Anschluss, for example, he ordered the construction of Austria's first concentration camp. Located near the village of Mauthausen, the camp overlooked a huge quarry where the inmates could cut stone for SS profit. Within a year or so, SS enterprises that relied mainly on concentration-camp labor were producing all manner of building materials, sewing uniforms for the Waffen-SS field troops, and at Himmler's request, experimenting with the medicinal qualities of herbs and other

foods. Inmates were even turning out the candlesticks that Himmler sent annually to the Lebensborn children who shared his birthday.

Himmler in 1939 created an SS agency, the Economic and Administrative Office, to oversee these enterprises. To direct it, he appointed Oswald Pohl, a shrewd administrator whose bull neck, bald pate, and overweening ambition reminded colleagues of the Italian dictator Mussolini. The SS businesses were registered as private companies, and the actual owner's identity shielded from the public. Behind this screen, Pohl and other officers found ways to exploit for personal gain the companies and the slave labor of the concentration camps. The case of the Sachsenhausen camp commandant who had a yacht built with inmate labor was unusual only in that he got caught. (Himmler himself was remarkably honest in matters of business, despite being chronically broke from supporting two families.)

In seeking to expand its economic empire in the occupied countries, the SS had to compete for the spoils with Göring's Four-Year Plan, the Ministry of Agriculture, and less powerful Nazi fiefdoms. To avoid a head-on clash with Göring, Himmler at times acquired fringe businesses. In the Sudetenland, for example, the SS gained a monopoly of mineral-water producers and started manufacturing furniture. The pickings were better in Poland. There the SS confiscated iron foundries, scores of cement works, and no fewer than 313 brick works—industries intended to provide materials for the enormous postwar housing and settlement program that Himmler envisioned in the East. The operation of many of these businesses was financed by big German companies such as I. G. Farben and Krupp, which were happy to supply Himmler with funds in exchange for his pledge of plentiful labor from the rapidly expanding web of concentration camps.

Even as Himmler was manipulating people and resources in Poland, a new arena for his energies opened farther east. Hitler's fateful decision to launch Operation Barbarossa—the invasion of the Soviet Union—on June 22, 1941, unleashed frenzied secret planning by SS technocrats. In their fantasies, planners in the Race and Settlement Central Office saw stretching across the steppes and woodlands of Russia a German empire so vast that it would dwarf the ambitious resettlement scheme still under way in Poland.

Their "master plan east" called for the Germanization of much of western Russia. Roughly 14 million of the inhabitants would be deported to Siberia and replaced by 2.4 million Germans. Although another 14 million Russians would be Germanized and allowed to remain, they would present no appreciable threat to the outnumbered newcomers. As envisioned by the SS planners, the German settlers would maintain control of their new colonial empire through a system of strongpoints. Each strongpoint would

Inmates in striped uniforms remove their caps in a required show of deference to a passing SS officer at the quarry of the Mauthausen concentration camp in Austria. Several additional camps were located near quarries to provide stone for the grandiose buildings the Nazis built to glorify their regime.

consist of a town of about 20,000 people surrounded by a ring of villages, each containing thirty to forty families of armed German farmers. Himmler thought this scenario "a sublime idea." Here, taking shape on paper, was his fantasy world of race and soil: pure-blooded German peasant warriors under the beneficent guidance of his beloved SS. Himmler even ordered scientists to start breeding a "winter-hardy steppe horse" that would not only serve as mount and beast of burden, but also furnish meat, milk, and cheese to his pioneers in the new Russian utopia.

Until Germany actually ruled the Soviet Union, however, Himmler could manipulate only a dream empire. And even when the Wehrmacht had penetrated deep into Russia, he knew there would be the inevitable skirmishing for power with Göring and other party rivals. In fact, before the

invasion, Adolf Hitler evidently decided to counter the growing power and greed of both Himmler and Göring. As his Reich minister for the East, ostensibly in charge of administering all the regions of Russia as they were conquered, he named neither Himmler nor Göring but instead Alfred Rosenberg, the longtime party ideologist who had once lived in Moscow.

All the same, Hitler entrusted the SS with awesome authority for the Russian campaign. Himmler was to operate independently behind the battlefronts, responsible only to the Führer himself, and was permitted to enlist the help of regular-army units when necessary. There, in the rear, his task forces of killers were to undertake what Hitler delicately labeled "special tasks for the preparation of the political administration."

Himmler's deputy Heydrich formed four task forces, designated with the letters A through D. They totaled about 3,000 men and a few women. Most of the officers were veteran SD, Gestapo, and Criminal Police agents selected for their ruthlessness. Much of the rank and file consisted of ordinary police officers and disciplinary cases from the Waffen-SS, some of whom volunteered for the job in order to escape punishment for infractions such as falling asleep on duty. The forces underwent three weeks of special training that included lectures on the inferiority of their "subhuman" targets, who were to be principally communist political commissars, gypsies, and Jews. It remains uncertain exactly when the Nazis settled on the annihilation of the Jews as the "final solution" to the questions of race that gnawed at their souls, but the decision was probably made early in the summer of 1941, and it was Hitler's to make.

The Einsatzgruppen followed the Wehrmacht into Russia on a front a thousand miles wide. They found their quarry everywhere—in urban ghettos, temporary prisoner-of-war camps, and peaceful villages. Each unit developed its own killing style. Otto Ohlendorf, commander of Task Force D in the southern sector, described a typical action carried out by his Einsatzgruppe: "The unit selected would enter a village or city and order the prominent Jewish citizens to call together all Jews for the purpose of resettlement. They were requested to hand over their valuables and, shortly before execution, to surrender their outer clothing. The men, women, and children were led to a place of execution, which in most cases was located next to a more deeply excavated antitank ditch. Then they were shot, kneeling or standing, and the corpses thrown into the ditch."

Reports of the slaughter piled up on the desk of Heydrich, who had returned to duty after flying with the Luftwaffe during the opening weeks of the invasion. Some accounts were couched in the evasive language of the bureaucracy—"disposed of," "rendered harmless," "seized." But from Lithuania, Task Force B reported bluntly that "about 500 Jews, among other

Following the pattern set in Poland, SS commandos prepare to hang five Russian civilians on a temporary gallows—just one of the means the Einsatzgruppen employed in the Soviet Union to eliminate "undesirables." The photograph was taken in 1941 by a German officer near the embattled city of Smolensk.

saboteurs, are currently being liquidated every day." And there were no euphemisms for what happened in Kiev on September 27 and 28: Ostensibly in reprisal for German casualties caused by the explosion of mines laid by the Red Army, 33,771 citizens—mostly Jews—were executed near the ravine called Babi Yar. At the end of 1941, Heydrich's statistics indicated that the task forces, with the help of local volunteer units in Latvia, Lithuania, Estonia, and the Ukraine, had killed nearly half a million people.

By such standards, the execution that took place in the city of Minsk a month or so after the invasion was a modest one. It was deemed special only by the presence of Heinrich Himmler. This extraordinary man, whom Hitler's architect Albert Speer later described as "half schoolmaster, half crank," wanted to see how the killing was done. He ordered the commander of Task Force B to line up 100 prisoners, men and women, and execute them. "When the first shots were heard and the victims collapsed, Himmler began to feel ill," an SS officer said later. "He reeled, almost fell to the ground, and then pulled himself together. Then he hurled abuse at the firing-squad members because of their poor marksmanship. Some of the women were still alive, for the bullets had simply wounded them."

Shaken by the experience, Himmler ordered his commanders to find a more humane method of mass killing. Soon the Einsatzgruppen were poisoning their prisoners in sealed trucks, custom-designed to direct the carbon-monoxide exhaust fumes to the victims within. The executioners grumbled, for the vans held no more than twenty-five people at a time, not nearly enough to kill on the scale ordered by Himmler and his henchmen. Clearly, the ways of extermination would have to be refined. ✚

A Painful Migration in Reverse

In September 1939, as Polish armies collapsed before the German blitzkrieg, Hitler assigned Reichsführer-SS Himmler to assimilate the far-flung *Volksdeutsche*, or ethnic Germans, into the new Reich. For centuries

Germans had migrated eastward, establishing enclaves reaching from the Baltic States to the Balkans to the fertile Russian heartland; by 1900 ethnic Germans in Russia alone numbered nearly two million. Wherever they went, the Volksdeutsche retained their language and customs. Now their perseverance would be tried anew as they left their adopted lands to confront an uncertain future in Greater Germany. Some of the émigrés, such as those from the Ukraine shown below, proceeded under armed escort.

The project gave Himmler the chance to test some of his cherished theories. Much of Poland would be cleansed of "biological enemies"—Slavs and Jews—to make room for the Volksdeutsche, whom Himmler envisioned as an "aristocracy of blood and soil." In fact, many of the 1.25 million ethnic Germans eventually transplanted were skeptical of the scheme and had to be prodded to leave their homes. Himmler chose to regard such intransigence as a good sign, asserting that it was "in the very nature of German blood to resist."

A German resident of Tariverte, Rumania, reads the local German-language newspaper to a neighbor in 1941. The headline announces the sinking of a thirteen-ship Allied convoy.

Traditionally clad women sit apart from the men in a Lutheran church in Transylvania. Of Rumania's 500,000 ethnic Germans, about 200,000 were relocated in Poland or Germany during the war's first two years.

A textile mill in Balzer near the Volga displays signs in Russian and German. In August 1941, two months after Germans crossed the Soviet border, Stalin exiled 379,000 Volga Volksdeutsche to inhospitable eastern Russia as "diversionists and spies."

Students do their homework beneath a bust of Lenin in the reading room of the central library of Marx, a German community in the Volga region.

Such schools, which yielded a literacy rate among ethnic Germans of nearly 100 percent, were far superior to those of native Russians.

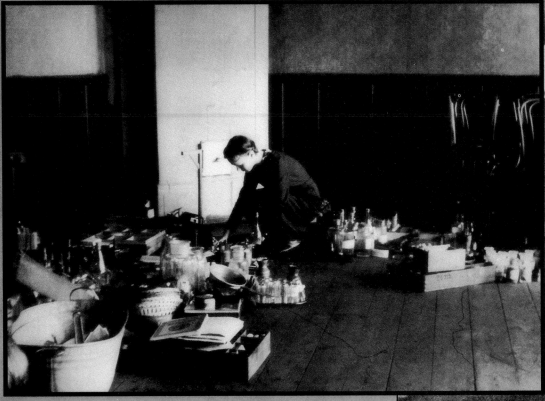

A German schoolteacher in the city of Riga, capital of the Baltic state of Latvia, packs her classroom supplies in preparation for resettlement in annexed Polish territory.

In a scene that was common in eastern Europe early in the war and likened by one witness to a glimpse "of the American frontier era," horse-drawn covered wagons carry ethnic Germans and their belongings along a desolate road to Hitler's Reich. Some wagon trains traveled as many as 2,000 miles.

Surrounded by their baggage at a
wharf in Riga, Latvian Germans
pass the time playing cards
while awaiting shipment to
Danzig, the free city on the Baltic
reclaimed by Germany in 1939.

A young newcomer to a resettlement camp near Chelmno in
occupied Poland receives a
picture of the Führer. The
numbered tags the people hold
identify each by family. All
arrivals were probed by SS
doctors and racial examiners to
see if they were fit to be
incorporated into the Reich.

Townspeople before an archway
emblazoned with the words
"Welcome to Greater Germany!"
salute Lithuanian Germans trek-
king into Eydtkau, on the East
Prussian border. Such demonstrations were deceptive; a Nazi
official noted that long stays
in resettlement camps left many
Volksdeutsche "disappointed,
embittered, and hopeless."

Schools for
a New Class
of Officers

In 1934 the fledgling armed branch of the SS—known as the SS-VT—embarked on a campaign to recruit officers from a broader field than that monopolized by Germany's regular army. True to its aristocratic Prussian heritage, the army sought officer candidates of good breeding who had graduated from at least a secondary school. The SS-VT, by contrast, offered advancement to promising candidates regardless of their education or social standing.

For an organization that could not yet boast of a glorious history, this proletarian approach was a virtue born of necessity. Those charged with grooming the new SS elite, however, set their sights high. They called their academies *Junkerschulen*, or schools for young nobles, and devised a curriculum to transform the sons of farmers and artisans into officers and gentlemen.

The prime mover behind this effort, retired Major General Paul Hausser, was the image of genteel authority. His approach was reflected in the sites chosen for the Junker schools. The gracious grounds of Bad Tölz *(right)*, for example, impressed on the cadets that, whatever their origins, they had been elevated to a lofty estate and must perform accordingly.

For some, this required basic training in matters that were not exclusively military. Incoming cadets were issued an etiquette manual that defined table manners ("Cutlery is held only with the fingers and not with the whole hand") and even contained instructions for closing a letter ("Heil Hitler! Yours sincerely, X"). Correct form was further encouraged through cultural activities and lectures on Nazi ideology. But the heart of the regimen was a bracing mixture of athletics and field exercises meant to yield Junkers who were nobly conditioned to command.

Idyllically set in the Bavarian Alps, Bad Tölz was one of two SS officer-training schools established before the war. Both were supervised by Paul Hausser, the Prussian-born inspector of the SS-VT, shown on the right in the inset conferring with the school's commandant.

Tutoring in Tactics and Wagner

The classroom challenges undertaken by SS officers-in-training ranged from playing war games in a sandbox to unraveling the meaning of Hitler's *Mein Kampf.* As a rule, ideology excited the cadets less than military theory; many had already been steeped in propaganda as members of the Hitler Youth. Nevertheless, ideology was an important factor in the examinations that eliminated one candidate in three during the five-month course. On one test the cadets were asked to expand on these words of Hitler: "The mixing of blood, and the sinking of the racial standard contingent upon this, is the sole cause for the demise of all cultures."

Stressing racial purity proved embarrassing during the war, when the Junker schools accepted recruits from occupied countries. Most foreigners enlisted to fight the Soviet Union, so the SS lecturers shifted from the sanctity of Nordic blood to the evils of Bolshevism.

Standing over a battle site that is reproduced in miniature on a sand table, a cadet *(right)* offers the solution to a tactical problem posed by his SS instructor *(left).*

In a university-like hall decked with swastikas, a ramrod-stiff instructor lectures on Nazi philosophy before a class of attentive student officers.

Broadening his cultural range, an aspiring officer in Braunschweig learns to play the organ at a Junker school, where such masters as Bach and Wagner dominated the curriculum.

Stress on Fitness and Mobility

A goal of the Junker schools was to produce officers who were fit to fight on the run. Building on mobile tactics introduced late in World War I, General Hausser prepared his cadets for rapid assaults that would leave the enemy reeling. This approach, according to Hausser's assistant, Colonel Felix Steiner, required "a supple, adaptable type of soldier, athletic of bearing, capable of more than average endurance."

To forge these soldier-athletes, the SS spared no expense. The facilities at Bad Tölz included a stadium for soccer and track-and-field events; separate halls for boxing, gymnastics, and indoor ball games; and a heated swimming pool and sauna. The complex attracted outstanding talent. At one time, eight of twelve coaches at Bad Tölz were national champions in their events.

A cadet parries his fencing opponent's thrust on a terrace at Bad Tölz. Himmler, who was infatuated with aristocratic customs, sanctioned duels with sword or pistol, decreeing that "every SS man has the right and the duty to defend his honor by force of arms."

The athletic program at Bad Tölz emphasized group exercises, such as lofting the medicine ball or tumbling through a human hoop *(right)*, as well as individual events, such as running the high hurdles *(above)*. The Junker schools enhanced their reputation by competing successfully against teams representing the army and the Luftwaffe.

137

An instructor points out a
landmark to a cadet during a
map-reading drill *(left)*, and
officer candidates launch an
amphibious attack *(above)* in
exercises that met the high
command's desire for mobility.

Girding Leaders to Thrive on Combat

Most of the prospects who entered the Junker schools were experienced men from the ranks of the SS, SA, or Gestapo who had been recommended by their commanding officers. Not all of the cadets, however, had been trained to the highest standard, and instruction during their early weeks at the Junker schools had to be devoted to handling weapons, clearing obstacle courses, and other fundamentals. After the basics, the candidates learned the advanced skills required of a small-unit commander, including field communications, coordinating infantry and artillery fire, and landing assault craft *(left)* on a hostile shore.

Always the aim was to produce leaders who were not cogs on a wheel, but versatile players in a mobile ensemble. The schools fostered a headlong combativeness that often paid big military dividends but sometimes led young officers to expose their units to unnecessary risks. And for all the Junkers' spirit, as SS men they remained political soldiers who might be called on to carry out orders that had no military justification.

Learning to lob grenades and hurdle fences prepared Junkers to share the perils of combat with their men. In the fighting to come, the 1938 graduates of Bad Tölz would suffer a fatality rate of 70 percent.

Absorbing the Art of Mountain War

As its combat role expanded during the war, the SS established two additional Junker schools, in Austria and Czechoslovakia, and a number of specialized training centers throughout occupied Europe. The demanding craft of mountain warfare was taught in a majestic arena—the Tyrolean Alps on the border of Austria and Italy.

To the school's first officer candidates, who arrived in 1942, the spectacular setting seemed a world away from the savage fighting in Russia and Africa. But the war was closing in on them. By 1943 the SS mountaineers had to interrupt their training to do battle with Italian partisans, who believed the time had come to send the Germans packing.

Cadets in the Tyrol simulate the rescue of a comrade. One man carries the casualty piggyback up a mountainside, and the two in the foreground act as counterweights on the towrope.

Dwarfed by 11,000-foot peaks, SS trainees aim a machine gun while their instructor

gazes over the valley below. Mountain-school graduates led troops against partisans and Americans in Italy.

Hitler's Private Army

F

ew commanders dared defy Adolf Hitler. Few thought so little of their lives. But Josef "Sepp" Dietrich was no ordinary officer. By the spring of 1940, the Führer's former bodyguard commanded the SS legion that bore Hitler's name—reason enough to swell a soldier's pride. He had shared with his master the struggle for power and won his highest praise: Hitler had even called him a national institution. If anyone had earned the right to question the Führer's judgment, it was Sepp Dietrich.

Thus on the evening of May 24, as the German armies on Hitler's orders ground to a grudging halt at the Aa Canal—just as they were about to crush the Allied forces at Dunkirk—Dietrich's crack Leibstandarte SS Adolf Hitler paused too, but only for the night. From the 230-foot heights across the canal, Allied observers could direct a torrent of artillery fire onto his exposed troops; Dietrich would have to move soon to save the men. The following morning—in defiance of Hitler's decree—Dietrich ordered the troops of his 3d Battalion across the canal. They climbed the hill and drove off the observers. For that act of disobedience, which might have cost another officer at least his rank, Dietrich was awarded the Knight's Cross of the Iron Cross. Not long afterward, a grateful Hitler shared his pleasure with all the Leibstandarte's members, telling them that henceforth "it will be an honor for you, who bear my name, to lead every German attack."

The Führer's vote of confidence was a milestone in the evolution of the Leibstandarte and its fellow units in Hitler's prized Waffen-, or military, SS. Troops of the SS were trying hard to refute their second-class status as parade-ground soldiers and their uneven combat performance in the conquest of Poland. Ahead lay a role in the fall of France and even greater glory in the Balkan campaign and invasion of Russia—a series of performances that would by the war's end earn the Waffen-SS a reputation as the "fire brigade" of the Third Reich.

If the Leibstandarte Adolf Hitler was the very heart of the Waffen-SS, then Sepp Dietrich was its soul. In 1941 the official SS journal *The Black Corps* trumpeted that Dietrich was "the father of his men ... the model for his

A battle-worn tank sergeant of the Waffen-SS Totenkopf Division, accompanied by panzer grenadiers, enters the Russian city of Kharkov in 1943. Pinned to his tunic are an infantry assault badge, an Iron Cross First Class, and a silver wound badge, indicating that he has been wounded more than twice.

unit commanders, a hard soldier with a strange, tender heart for his comrades . . . vassal of Adolf Hitler . . . a knight without fear and without reproach." It was Dietrich who had answered Hitler's call for a household guard in March of 1933. He formed the Sonderkommando Berlin, or Special Detail for Berlin, 120 SS men, handpicked not only to protect the Führer, but also—as phrased in Hermann Göring's malignant parlance—to complete "other assignments."

Years would pass before this praetorian guard would mature into the elite corps that would make all of Europe tremble, and years more before Himmler would rechristen that corps the Waffen-SS, but already the die was cast. Within months of its inception, the Sonderkommando Berlin had been redesignated the Leibstandarte SS Adolf Hitler, thus ensuring the avid attention of its namesake. On the evening of November 9, 1933—the tenth anniversary of the failed Beer Hall Putsch—the Leibstandarte, now 800 strong, gathered in the Bavarian capital of Munich for a ceremony that confirmed the special nature of the unit's relationship with the Führer. There, as quaking torchlight played on the walls of the Feldherrnhalle, members of the regiment swore allegiance to Hitler, pledging loyalty to him alone and "obedience unto death."

Dietrich's Leibstandarte did not have to wait long to demonstrate its loyalty. In June of 1934 it was tapped for grisly duty on the Night of the Long Knives, the purge that cost Ernst Röhm and other fractious leaders of the SA their lives. As a reward for his "distinguished service" in the suppression of the SA, Sepp Dietrich was promoted to *SS-Obergruppenführer*, or lieutenant general, on July 5, 1934; like other participants in the purge, he was sworn to silence regarding all he had seen and done throughout that night and in the days that followed.

A few months later, in September 1934, Hitler took a giant step toward building a military wing of the party by approving the formation of the SS Verfügungstruppe, or SS-VT, special-service troops at Hitler's disposal, including his pet Leibstandarte. The SS-VT provided the seed from which a future SS division could grow. While the Führer's order raised a number of eyebrows in the German army, another Hitler directive the following spring heightened concerns around the world: He announced that military conscription, banned in Germany by the Versailles treaty, would be reinstated and that Germany would build an army of thirty-six divisions, several times as many as the treaty allowed. A year later, in March 1936, Hitler sent the world another message when German forces, including elements of the Leibstandarte, reoccupied the Rhineland.

Despite the threat the SS-VT posed to its monopoly, the army was successful for a time in keeping a leash on the growth of its rival. The army

was the main supply line for the SS-VT, its sole source of weapons and of much-needed military training. Even more important, the army was able to control the flow of recruits into the SS-VT through the Reich's network of Wehrbezirkskommandos, or WBKs. These local draft boards were responsible for calling up conscripts and assigning them to the various branches of the armed forces based on quotas set by the OKW, the German high command. Thus limiting the size of the armed SS was a simple matter of assigning it a relatively low quota—or so the generals of the high command convinced themselves.

But in their complacence the generals underestimated the resolve of Heinrich Himmler to create a powerful private army. Himmler formed two new militarized SS regiments, Germania and Deutschland, which together with the Leibstandarte Adolf Hitler and a communications detachment, composed the SS-VT. Himmler was determined that these new units not become the object of ridicule the Leibstandarte had been in its early days, when it was scorned as an outfit of ceremonial guards who looked smart on review but were no match for a genuine fighting force. Toward that end, the SS had established an officer-training school at Bad Tölz and another at Braunschweig. Both of these *Junkerschulen* relied on regular-army training methods and the firm hand of former Reichswehr officers to groom their cadets to combat readiness. The candidates had to meet stringent requirements before ever setting foot on academy grounds. No SS officer could stand shorter than five feet ten inches, for example, and candidates for the Leibstandarte had to be an inch taller than that.

On October 1, 1936, Himmler tapped the commandant at Braunschweig, Paul Hausser, to become inspector of the SS-VT with the rank of *Brigadeführer*, or brigadier general. In his new post, Hausser set out to apply to the entire Verfügungstruppe the methods that had worked in the officer-training schools. In the process he gradually shaped the SS-VT into a creditable force in the image of the exalted Wehrmacht, the regular armed services of the new Reich. Indeed, by late 1937 Himmler could announce with unrestrained pride that "the Verfügungstruppe is, according to the present standards of the Wehrmacht, prepared for war."

Although Hausser was succeeding in the formidable task of molding the SS-VT for combat, the prickly independence of Sepp Dietrich was causing him no end of problems. The personality clash between the upstart Dietrich and the dour, demanding Hausser was aggravated by the fact that for all his military experience, Hausser was outranked in the SS by the diminutive former army sergeant with the peasant background. Just as galling were Dietrich's easy access to the Führer and the Leibstandarte's honored place in Hitler's private pantheon. Even Himmler complained that the Leibstandarte was "a complete law unto itself." At one point Hausser became so frustrated by Dietrich's intractability that he threatened to resign and mockingly proposed that Himmler put Dietrich in command of the SS-VT. In time, however, Dietrich grew more amenable as he realized that Hausser's training and organizational skills were giving the SS-VT a luster that even the Wehrmacht was beginning to notice.

For all his reputation as a swashbuckling paladin, Dietrich paled alongside Theodor Eicke, a "self-styled prince" of the SS, as a Nazi colleague described him. The one-time army paymaster and police informer had, like Dietrich, climbed quickly to a position of importance in the SS. Eicke had joined the Nazi party only five years before Himmler appointed him commandant at the Dachau concentration camp in 1933. That same year, Eicke had formed the first SS Totenkopfverbände, or Death's-Head units. These guard detachments became the nucleus of the Totenkopf, or SS-T, another element of the future Waffen-SS.

Eicke's career had reached a turning point on July 1, 1934, when he shared the dubious honor of dispatching Ernst Röhm. Four days later Eicke was appointed inspector of the Reich's concentration-camp system and made head of its guard formations. A week after that, he was promoted to SS major general, the second-highest commissioned rank in the SS; during the following year he took advantage of his new position to consolidate his power and to transform his widely scattered guard units into an armed force that rivaled the SS-VT.

But where the SS-VT took pride from the beginning in its elitism, the SS-T

relished its ruthlessness. Eicke's Death's-Head units were magnets for the uneducated, the unemployed, and the unscrupulous, constituting what one observer described as an "army of thugs." Eicke seemed to prefer it that way and railed against any "ludicrous attempt to ape a military organization." In 1937 Eicke issued an order declaring that the Totenkopf units "belong neither to the army nor to the police nor to the Verfügungstruppe." Like Dietrich, however, even Eicke eventually came to change his style and grudgingly remolded the SS Totenkopf regiments along regular-army lines.

Handling the likes of Dietrich and Eicke was no easy task, but fortunately for Hausser there were at his disposal a number of former regular-army officers who proved more disciplined and professional. One of the most influential was Felix Steiner. Like Hausser, he was a World War I veteran who had seen firsthand the futility of trench warfare. What was needed, Steiner reasoned, was a highly mobile, highly disciplined fighting force whose lightning-fast operations "would split the enemy into fragments and then destroy the dislocated remnants."

Appointed commander of the Munich-based SS regiment Deutschland, Steiner worked to turn military theory into practice, introducing a number of innovations that were adopted throughout the military SS. For example, Steiner created small, mobile battle groups that could respond to any exigency on a moment's notice. He armed some of his men with submachine guns and grenades instead of rifles for greater firepower, and dressed them in newly designed camouflage suits for better concealment. On the training ground he shifted the emphasis from marching drills to competitive sports in an effort to create a cadre of military athletes motivated by a distinctive esprit de corps. Steiner's dynamic methods understandably attracted the attention of his superiors and eventually made him Himmler's "favorite baby," as Hausser somewhat caustically put it.

On August 17, 1938, Hitler served notice that his armed SS was destined to be more than merely a private police force. He authorized the motorization of the SS-VT and decreed—no doubt to the dismay of the Wehrmacht generals—that it would both fight in the coming war and enforce the Nazi-dominated peace that was sure to follow. Under the terms of his decree, the SS-VT and SS Totenkopfverbände were to be prepared for use both in "special internal political tasks" and in the event of mobilization for war. As long as the peace held, the armed SS was to report to Himmler and to continue drawing its weapons and equipment from the Wehrmacht. Once war broke out, SS forces would be at the disposal of either Himmler or the army's commander in chief, as the Führer saw fit. Even when they served under the auspices of the army, the troops would "remain politically

RANK	COLLAR	RANK	COLLAR
Reichsführer-SS *(No U.S. Equivalent)*		**SS-Obersturmführer** *First Lieutenant*	
SS-Oberstgruppenführer *General*		**SS-Untersturmführer** *Second Lieutenant*	
SS-Obergruppenführer *Lieutenant General*		**SS-Sturmscharführer** *Sergeant Major*	
SS-Gruppenführer *Major General*		**SS-Hauptscharführer** *Master Sergeant*	
SS-Brigadeführer *Brigadier General*		**SS-Oberscharführer** *Technical Sergeant*	
SS-Oberführer *(No U.S. Equivalent)*		**SS-Scharführer** *Staff Sergeant*	
SS-Standartenführer *Colonel*		**SS-Unterscharführer** *Sergeant*	
SS-Obersturmbannführer *Lieutenant Colonel*		**SS-Rottenführer** *Acting Corporal*	
SS-Sturmbannführer *Major*		**SS-Oberschütze** *Private First Class*	
SS-Hauptsturmführer *Captain*		**SS-Schütze** *Private*	

an arm of the Nazi party." The SS-VT would also continue to be financed by the Ministry of the Interior, although the German high command would be permitted to scrutinize the SS-VT's budget.

Hitler's decree stipulated that service in the SS-VT would satisfy a young German's military obligation, although service in the SS-T would not. And the decree strengthened the heretofore tenuous link between the SS-VT and the SS-T by specifying that in the event of war, some units of the SS-T were to be used as a reserve pool for the SS-VT, which lacked its own reserve. Other SS-T units would be mobilized as a "police force" to be deployed at Himmler's whim. In peacetime, however, the SS-T would continue to perform duties of a "police nature"—guarding concentration camps, for example—and would have no outward affiliation with the SS-VT.

For all the training and preparation, the armed SS had yet to test its mettle in combat. There were two opportunities in 1938. In March a motorized battalion of Dietrich's Leibstandarte had accompanied Wehrmacht troops occupying Austria during the Anschluss. But the Austrians had failed to fight back. Likewise, three SS-VT regiments and two battalions of SS-T participated in the occupation of the Czech Sudetenland in the autumn and met no resistance. An order issued by the OKW, congratu-

To distinguish its officers and enlisted personnel from those of the Wehrmacht, the SS maintained its own hierarchy of ranks. Listed above with their American army equivalents, they range from the *SS-Schütze,* or private, to Reichsführer-SS, a category reserved for Himmler.

lating the troops following the Sudetenland operation, pointedly neglected to mention the role of the SS. Hitler, on reading a draft of the order, insisted that it be rewritten to include his pet forces in the praise.

Not until Poland was overrun in the late summer of 1939 did the SS forces receive their trial by fire. In preparation for the invasion, on August 19 Hitler mobilized a number of SS units, including Steiner's Deutschland Regiment and Dietrich's Leibstandarte SS Adolf Hitler, and ordered them attached to various regular-army commands. With war imminent, it grew to be time for the SS to prove it could fight in the field as impressively as it had marched through the streets and squares of Munich and Berlin. Himmler bade farewell to his special soldiers with a paternal admonition: "SS men, I expect you to do more than your duty."

As it happened, events in Poland left the combat effectiveness of the SS troops in grave doubt. Their willingness to fight was never in question— in fact, they seemed in some cases almost too eager. The German high command, which not surprisingly chose to downplay the role of the SS in Poland, reported that the SS units had acted recklessly on the battlefield, exposing themselves to unnecessary risk and incurring proportionally heavier losses than the Wehrmacht troops. Moreover, the OKW contended, the SS was poorly trained and its officers woefully unsuited to command men in the heat of battle. Indeed, much to the embarrassment of the SS, Dietrich's Leibstandarte had to be rescued by an infantry regiment after the SS soldiers found themselves surrounded by Polish forces at Pabianice.

In its defense, the SS argued that it had been improperly equipped by the Wehrmacht and hampered by orders to fight piecemeal in units under the control of unfamiliar Wehrmacht commanders. Such excuses failed to placate the generals. In the wake of the Polish invasion, they sought to disband the SS-VT but failed to sway Hitler. In the meantime, Himmler lobbied for greater autonomy for his forces, insisting that they be allowed to fight in their own divisions, under their own commanders, and with their own weapons and supply services.

Hitler, unwilling to anger his army generals further and equally reluctant to ruffle his SS chief, chose a middle course. He allowed the SS to form its own divisions, as Himmler had requested, but placed those divisions under army command in combat. Accordingly, in early October 1939, three SS-VT regiments—Deutschland, Germania, and Der Führer—were reorganized as the SS Verfügungs Division. The remaining SS-VT regiment, the Leibstandarte SS Adolf Hitler, became a reinforced motorized regiment, but was intentionally omitted from the Verfügungs Division so that later it could be expanded into another division. In addition, there were to be two new field divisions: the SS Totenkopf Division, comprising elements of the SS-T under

the command of Eicke, and the SS Polizei Division, formed from the ranks of the Nazi regime's uniformed police force.

Suddenly—and to the alarm of the generals—what had been a force of about 18,000 soldiers at the outset of the Polish invasion was now a unit 100,000 strong. Moreover, to protect his new divisions from Wehrmacht interference, Himmler had persuaded the Führer to institute special SS courts to try wayward SS personnel, effectively removing the SS from the legal jurisdiction of the German army.

The development could not have been timelier from Himmler's viewpoint. Already an SS man had been court-martialed for his role in the shooting of fifty Polish Jews. Himmler wanted to make sure that such a trial would not be repeated, especially now that some Wehrmacht officers were complaining about the murderous rear-guard activities of the SS in Poland.

In his ceaseless efforts to achieve autonomy for his troops, Himmler was aided by his glib and clever recruiting chief, Gottlob Berger. Using formidable negotiating skills, Berger extracted an agreement from OKW that established an independent support network to provide recruitment, supply, administration, justice, welfare, weapons-development, and medical services. These services would be staffed by the SS, not the Wehrmacht. In another concession to Berger, the German high command allowed the SS to establish reserve formations for its field divisions. Since Himmler was given total authority over the reserves, he could use them throughout

Sympathizers hail the soldiers of the Waffen-SS as they ride down an Amsterdam street following the surrender of the Netherlands on May 14, 1940. The parade was part of a motorized grand tour of the nation in which German troops, appearing none the worse for their lightning conquest of Holland, sought to overawe the populace.

occupied Europe in various "police activities," freeing the SS-T units usually assigned such duties for subsequent incorporation into the armed SS.

Himmler gave his military units the collective title Waffen-SS, from *Waffe*, the German word for weapon. Now he faced the problem of equipping his growing legions. Hitler complicated the arms situation enormously in March 1940, when he authorized the formation of four new motorized artillery battalions to be attached to the Waffen-SS divisions and Dietrich's Leibstandarte. Although the Wehrmacht was supposed to provide arms for the SS, the high command now proved exceedingly reluctant to dip into its arsenal. Only slowly did the OKW consent to supply the Waffen-SS with artillery. By the time of the invasion of the West, the Leibstandarte's new artillery battalion had received the weapons it needed—no doubt because of Dietrich's favored status. But the other units went begging.

In an effort to open the supply bottleneck, Heinrich Gärtner, head of the SS Procurement Office, attempted to bypass the army's distribution system by dealing directly with the newly formed Reich Ministry for Arms and Munitions. During a meeting with the armaments minister, Fritz Todt, Gärtner presented an SS shopping list that included thousands of small arms, hundreds of artillery pieces, and millions of rounds of ammunition. Unflustered by the enormity of the request, Todt assured Gärtner of his cooperation, albeit for a price—20,000 Polish laborers who could be put to work in the Reich's weapons factories.

Not content with the arms channel he appeared to have opened through Todt, Gärtner also arranged to procure a shipment of smoke grenades directly from the manufacturer. This affront to OKW authority, coupled with the proposed Todt pipeline, was too much for the generals to ignore. On June 18, 1940, the SS was informed that the OKW would under no circumstances countenance a "private supply organization" and that as long as the Waffen-SS was attached to the Wehrmacht it would get what it needed through army channels. The OKW directive spelled the end to Gärtner's plan for an SS supply conduit. Himmler's army had lost an important round in its fight for autonomy.

As Himmler and his aides worked behind the scenes to enlarge their fiefdom, troops of the Waffen-SS were feverishly preparing for war in the West. Attached to army commands, SS units spent the late winter and spring of 1940 training for combat. At the same time, the Reich's strategists were plotting and replotting their plan of attack, a plan that ultimately took the code name *Fall Gelb*, or Case Yellow.

In its final form, German strategy called for one army group to sweep through Holland and Belgium in a diversionary attack that would lure

Allied forces northward while a second army group drove through the Ardennes and into the heart of France, annihilating the British Expeditionary Force and at least part of the French army. Meanwhile, a third army group would feint against the Maginot line farther south, keeping its garrisons occupied. The three army groups would join to capture Paris and finish off the French forces.

Early in the month of May the army moved into position on Germany's western border, the SS units deploying alongside the regular forces. The Leibstandarte, attached to the 227th Infantry Division, and one regiment of the Verfügungs Division, Der Führer, waited near the Dutch border. The rest of the Verfügungs Division massed near Münster in Westfalen, where it awaited the signal to invade the Netherlands once the country's border had been breached, while the Totenkopf and Polizei divisions were held in reserve in Germany.

On the evening of May 9, 1940, the code word *Danzig* was flashed to the 136 divisions in the attack force. The following morning, as daylight's first hues filtered into Holland, German tanks, planes, and infantry roared across the border. Blitzkrieg had begun.

In the German spearhead, the Leibstandarte Adolf Hitler quickly overcame Dutch border guards near the town of De Poppe, then pushed on toward the Ijssel River, one of its motorcycle companies penetrating forty-eight miles in just five hours without encountering resistance. Meanwhile, Der Führer crossed the Ijssel near Arnhem with the 207th Infantry Division and rolled toward Utrecht.

The following morning, the SS Verfügungs Division, commanded by Hausser, crossed the Meuse River with the 9th Panzer Division and pressed toward Moerdijk and Rotterdam. With Dutch resistance crumbling before the sudden German onslaught of men and metal, British and French armies sped north in order to relieve the pressure on their besieged Dutch allies, just as the German strategists had hoped. Consequently, on the morning of May 11 the 9th Panzer and SS Verfügungs divisions collided head-on with the French Seventh Army under General Henri Giraud near the Dutch town of Tilburg. The impact sent the French force reeling, and within three days Giraud's army had withdrawn from the Netherlands and redeployed in Belgium.

The 9th Panzer and Verfügungs divisions continued their push through Holland, now reinforced by Dietrich's Leibstandarte, and on the afternoon of May 12 the German tanks rolled into the outskirts of Rotterdam on the North Sea. There they were stopped cold by stubborn Dutch resistance. Two days later, with the German advance on the city still stalled, Hitler and Göring decided to bomb Rotterdam into submission. The subsequent raid,

which lasted only fifteen terrifying minutes, flattened the city center and took the lives of more than 800 Dutch civilians. Two hours later the defenders of Rotterdam surrendered.

In the wake of the capitulation, Dietrich's Leibstandarte threaded through the streets of Rotterdam. Nearby, General Kurt Student, the founder and commander of Germany's paratroop corps, was setting up his command post in the recently vacated Dutch military headquarters. Passing the building, Dietrich's SS men saw armed Dutch soldiers gathered outside but failed to notice that the enemy troops were disarming themselves in accordance with the terms of surrender. The trigger-happy Leibstandarte sprayed the hapless Dutch soldiers with machine-gun fire. When General Student stepped to the window to investigate the shooting, a stray German bullet struck him in the head.

Though severely wounded, Student survived his encounter with the Leibstandarte. The SS troops sped onward toward Delft and The Hague, unaware that they had almost killed one of Germany's finest generals. Dietrich's men had scarcely left Rotterdam when General Henri Gerard Winkelman, the commander in chief of all Dutch forces, capitulated to the Germans. Nevertheless, the Leibstandarte swept on, netting some 3,500 Dutch prisoners before it reached The Hague on May 15 and learned of Holland's formal surrender.

By May 24 the German regular army and Waffen-SS forces had squeezed the Allied armies into an ever-constricting pocket around the French seaport of Dunkirk on the English Channel. The Leibstandarte, having rushed westward to join General Heinz Guderian's XIX Panzer Corps, now stood on the Aa Canal facing the Allied line of defense near Watten, just fifteen miles southwest of Dunkirk. To the southeast, a thirty-two-man patrol from the SS Verfügungs Division had bridged the canal and penetrated another five miles, only to be surrounded by enemy tanks and then destroyed after a valiant last stand. Undaunted, other units of the Verfügungs Division successfully crossed the canal and established a bridgehead at Saint Venant, thirty miles from Dunkirk.

As night fell, the German high command issued Hitler's controversial order that, for the moment, brought an end to the German advance. It was the next morning that Dietrich, his men dangerously exposed to Allied artillery fire directed from the opposite heights, defied the Führer's order and crossed the canal to seize the high ground.

On that same day British troops succeeded in pushing the Verfügungs Division out of Saint Venant; it was the first time in the Western offensive that any SS unit had been forced to relinquish ground it had taken. That setback was followed by a near disaster on May 28, when an isolated British stronghold opened fire on Dietrich's staff car as it was passing by. The gunfire ignited the vehicle's fuel tank and forced Dietrich and his adjutant to scramble into a roadside ditch. From there the two managed to crawl into a nearby culvert, which offered protection from the rain of enemy bullets but left them vulnerable to the seepage of burning gasoline that was even then entering their shelter. Smearing themselves with mud to ward off the heat of the flames, they huddled in the culvert for the next five hours until the Leibstandarte's 3d Battalion arrived and rescued them.

The German advance resumed on May 26. By May 28 elements of the Leibstandarte had captured from British forces the village of Wormhout, which lay ten miles from Dunkirk. The day before, farther south, the SS regiment Deutschland commanded by the redoubtable Steiner reached the Allied defensive line on the Lys Canal at the village of Merville. During the afternoon Steiner forged a bridgehead on the Allied side of the canal and waited for the Totenkopf Division and the 3d Panzer Division to arrive and cover his flanks before his regiment pushed on. During an inspection of the bridgehead that evening, Steiner and his adjutant heard what they assumed was the welcome rumble of German panzer treads, only to realize in horror that a menacing column of about twenty British tanks had penetrated their position. Steiner's men fought suicidally, holding their ground as the enemy tanks rolled to within fifteen feet of them. Steiner saw one SS officer heroically defend himself and his comrades with hand grenades before being crushed by a tank. An *SS-Schütze*, or private, clambered atop one of the advancing tanks in a futile attempt to slip a hand grenade through its observation slit. In the end, only the timely arrival of a tank-destroyer platoon from the Totenkopf Division prevented Deutschland from being swept from its bridgehead.

Fritz Knöchlein, former officer of guards at Dachau, commanded the Totenkopf troops who gunned down some 100 British prisoners at Le Paradis, France, on May 27, 1940. The massacre took place on Knöchlein's twenty-ninth birthday.

As would happen again among other SS units later in the war, the display of valor exhibited by the regiment Deutschland was offset by an atrocity committed elsewhere on the same day. As the Totenkopf Division advanced in the vicinity of Merville, encountering stubborn British resistance, a company led by Lieutenant Fritz Knöchlein surrounded a farmhouse being used as a strongpoint by soldiers of the 2d Royal Norfolk. Determined to stall the German advance and buy time for their comrades' escape, the Britons kept the air alive with bullets for almost an hour. Then, with their ammunition spent and entertaining no hope of rescue, 100 men of the 2d

Norfolk raised a white flag and marched out of the house to what they expected would be captivity.

On Knöchlein's orders, the surrendering British soldiers were first searched. Then, as they filed past a barn wall, they were cut down by the raking crossfire of a pair of machine guns. Those who survived were shot at close range or bayoneted before the SS troops left the scene of the atrocity. Buried within the heap of dead and dying, however, were two British soldiers who lived not only to tell their tale after the war, but to see Knöchlein hang for his crime.

By May 30 most of the British Expeditionary Force and its French and Belgian partners had retreated to Dunkirk, and many had been spirited off the coast to safety in England. The major battles of the German invasion had been fought. Waffen-SS units participated next in the drive to capture Paris, then plunged southward in the forefront of the German pursuit of the remnants of the French army. It was more of a chase than a fight—most of the dispirited French troops surrendered without making a stand. By June 24 the Leibstandarte, having sliced deeper into France than any other German unit, had arrived in Saint Etienne, located 250 miles to the south of Paris. The next day the fighting ended. After only six weeks of battle, the Germans had conquered the West.

While the Wehrmacht's pride in its accomplishments soared, the OKW continued to ignore the battlefield contributions of the Waffen-SS, whose acknowledgment was left to Hitler. In the course of a speech to the Reichstag on July 19, 1940, the Führer praised all the German forces that had participated in the western campaign, but he singled out for special acclaim "the valiant divisions and regiments of the Waffen-SS," which, together with the German Armored Corps, had "inscribed for itself a place in the history of the world."

The Führer's speech helped immeasurably to reinforce the notion that the Waffen-SS was a singularly elite military organization—as Hitler characterized it, "superiority personified, inspired by a fierce will." But if Hitler's words of praise polished the military reputation of the Waffen-SS in the Reich, they made little impression on the OKW, nor did they secure the high command's cooperation with Himmler's minions. Indeed, as the SS was earning respect during the battle for France, in Berlin Berger was complaining to Himmler that the persistently balky Wehrbezirkskommandos were holding up the processing of 15,000 SS recruits. "The trouble," fumed Berger, "is that the Führer's orders are never completely carried out, but are halted halfway."

Doggedly, Berger continued to plead for recruits, especially after Hitler's surprise revelation to intimates in midsummer that the Soviet Union, not

NEDERLANDERS

VOOR UW EER EN GEWETEN OP! - TEGEN HET BOLSJEWISME DE WAFFEN ⚡⚡ ROEPT U!

Reaching Out for Foreign Legions

THE WAFFEN-SS CALLS YOU! That summons, spelled out boldly on the Dutch poster above, was repeated in more than a dozen languages during the Second World War as Heinrich Himmler's expanding corps sought fresh manpower in the occupied countries. As illustrated here and on the pages that follow, SS recruiting posters capitalized on the German invasion of the Soviet Union in 1941 by encouraging able-bodied men from Brussels to Belgrade to join in a crusade against communism.

Whether they signed up in order to fight Bolsheviks or simply to fight, those who volunteered were flattered to be portrayed as patriots whose native traditions would be honored by their SS officers. Few recruits harbored that illusion for long, however. The largely Catholic Flemish recruits from Belgium, for instance, were dismayed to learn that the SS would not let them celebrate mass in camp, and they were shocked when their German sergeants derided them as a "race of gypsies" and a "nation of idiots."

Below, a Waffen-SS soldier doubles as a Viking warrior in a recruiting poster that urged "Norsemen" to do battle for Norway. Proceeding clockwise from lower left, the other posters exhort French citizens to protect their homeland, Danes to crush Bolshevism, Bosnian Muslims and Croatian Christians to trample on the Red flag, Flemish patriots to stand up for the Belgian emblem, and French-speaking Belgians to do the same by joining the fight on the Eastern Front.

England, would be the Reich's next target for invasion. By August 1940, after calculating the projected invasion's cost in troops, Berger sought Himmler's permission to expand the Waffen-SS by setting up recruiting offices in the recently conquered countries, thus tapping "the German and Germanic population not at the disposal of the Wehrmacht." In fact, the welcome mat had been laid out for such racially pure foreigners since early 1940; already the SS counted among its legions a few volunteers in possession "of Nordic blood," including forty-four from Switzerland, three from Sweden, and five from the United States.

Hitler had reservations about recruiting foreigners. He sensed that any increase in the size of the Waffen-SS would further alienate his regular-army generals; moreover, the addition of foreigners blemished his vision of an SS coursing with only "the best German blood." Nevertheless, swayed by the presentations of Heinrich Himmler and Gottlob Berger, who argued that it would be better for young Europeans to invest their energy in the SS than in anti-German resistance groups, Hitler approved the formation of a new SS division, to be recruited mostly from foreign nationals. By June of 1940 Himmler had authorized the enlistment of Danish and Norwegian volunteers into the newly formed SS regiment Nordland and the induction of Dutch and Belgian volunteers into the SS regiment Westland—the first two regiments of the new division and the first of many SS units to consist in part of foreign volunteers. Enlistments poured in at such a rapid rate that by the end of the year the SS had established a training camp at Sennheim, in Alsace-Lorraine, that was exclusively for its non-German recruits.

Undeterred by Hitler's reservations, Heinrich Himmler pressed tirelessly to expand further the dimensions and the power of his realm. He won approval to give the Waffen-SS its own high command—the SS Führungshauptamt—to rival those of the other services. He arranged for Waffen-SS troops to exchange whatever old captured enemy weapons they had been using for new arms that were manufactured in Germany. In addition, he began to shift to the Waffen-SS control of the Totenkopf regiments—some police reservists and the guard units spawned by the Reich's growing network of concentration camps—in order to convert them to front-line infantry regiments and enlarge his fighting forces. In the process, he dissolved the headquarters unit that had operated the concentration camps and transferred its responsibilities to the new high command of the

Bosnian Muslims in death's-head fezzes examine a tract on Islam and Jewry at their camp in Yugoslavia in 1943. Himmler glibly denied the Slavic heritage of these recruits, portraying them as descendants of Goths who once overran the region.

Waffen-SS. This administrative move would return to haunt the Waffen-SS later. The soldiers of this elite force, often honored for their spirit and gallantry on the battlefield, would be irrevocably tainted by association with the torturers and exterminators who ran the concentration camps, and the price to be paid would be costly when moral debts were settled in the years following the war.

But in the aftermath of its triumphant march through France, the Waffen-SS appeared to be destined only for glory. By the beginning of 1941 it had grown to six divisions, had been reorganized and refitted, and was prepared for its next test. The challenge came, however, not with the invasion of the Soviet Union as Adolf Hitler had planned, but elsewhere—and entirely as a result of the unwitting interference of Benito Mussolini in the Führer's grand plan.

Without consulting his Axis ally in Berlin, Mussolini in October 1940 sent the Italian army into Greece. Hitler called it a "regrettable blunder," made more lamentable by the subsequent defeats of the Italians. Worse yet, British forces were rushing to the aid of the Greek army, creating a dangerous situation that Hitler could not ignore.

Accordingly, Hitler's strategists devised a plan, code-named Operation Marita, to invade and secure Greece. But before their scheme could be translated into action, it was upset by developments elsewhere in the Balkans; the government of Yugoslavia, only days after signing an agreement with the Axis powers, was toppled by a military revolt and replaced by an anti-German regime. Hitler, incensed, was compelled to add Yugoslavia to his invasion plan.

Soon afterward, the SS division Reich departed France and started for Rumania, its staging area, while the Leibstandarte SS Adolf Hitler, which had been reinforced to brigade strength, rolled toward Bulgaria. Along the way, the SS units jousted repeatedly, not with Allied enemies, but with their German army counterparts. These skirmishes were bloodless, for the most part involving rights of way on traffic-snarled roads, but they underscored the ill will between the two branches of the service. In one incident an SS officer threatened to have his men open fire on an army convoy if it dared to pass his vehicles. On another occasion an SS officer brought to a halt an army convoy that had overtaken his column, then had the lead army vehicle held at gunpoint, with mines placed beneath its front wheels, until the SS had cleared the area.

The real fighting began on the morning of April 6, 1941, when German armor and infantry poured into Yugoslavia and Greece. The Leibstandarte Adolf Hitler, attached to General Georg Stumme's XL Panzer Corps, moved west from the Bulgarian border, then turned to the south and pushed

Armored cars pace the advance of the Leibstandarte Adolf Hitler through the Balkans in the spring of 1941. Attached to the German army's XL Corps, the Leibstandarte fought its way from Sofia, Bulgaria, to Athens, Greece, in less than a month.

through mountainous terrain toward Greece. By April 9, having met little resistance, Dietrich's brigade had reached the town of Prilep, just thirty miles from the Greek frontier.

Far to the north, the SS division Reich, advancing with General Georg-Hans Reinhardt's XLI Panzer Corps, struck across the Rumanian border toward the Yugoslav capital of Belgrade, which had already been pounded into rubble by the Luftwaffe. Arriving there on April 12, an advance party of the SS division accepted the city's capitulation. A few days later, the Yugoslav army surrendered.

The Leibstandarte had crossed into Greece and was fighting southward through a strategically important pass near the town of Vevi. The defile was defended by elements of a British Expeditionary Force under Lieutenant General Sir Henry Wilson. The British commander was determined to slow, if not stop, the German thrust, making the invading unit pay dearly for every inch of ground it gained.

For forty-eight hours, from April 10 to 12, the Leibstandarte slowly fought

Savoring victory in Greece, the Leibstandarte assembles in an ancient stadium at Olympia. The troops had fought so well, declared SS General Kurt Daluege, that their critics "must change their opinions once and for all."

through the pass until the brigade reached the foot of a hill that was later designated Height 997. From this elevated vantage point, Wilson's artillery observers could watch the Germans' every move; capture of the promontory was essential if the SS brigade was to advance. Dietrich sent his 1st Company, led by Lieutenant Gert Pleiss, to storm the hill, and in the ensuing bloody hand-to-hand fighting with Australians of the 6th Division, his troops prevailed. The capture of Height 997 opened the way through the pass and allowed the Germans into the heart of Greece. To the gratification of the Waffen-SS, Dietrich's victory finally evoked the congratulations of the Wehrmacht. In his order for the day, General Stumme thanked the SS troops, commended them for their "unshakable offensive spirit," and concluded resoundingly that "the present victory signifies for the Leibstandarte a new and imperishable page of honor in its history. Forward for Führer, Volk, and Reich!"

Forward the Leibstandarte went, racing through the pass and beyond. The next day, the unit's reconnaissance battalion, led by Major Kurt Meyer, veered southwest from the mountain channel and ran into stiff opposition from Greek troops defending yet another mountain defile, the Klisura Pass. At one point in the fighting, Meyer and an advance party found themselves trapped under heavy machine-gun fire. To prevent his men from being slaughtered in their exposed position, Meyer ordered them forward but received no response. He decided that only drastic action would persuade the troops to run the gauntlet of gunfire. As Meyer later recalled the moment, he grabbed a hand grenade and shouted to attract the attention of his men: "Everybody looks thunderstruck at me as I brandish the grenade, pull the pin, and roll it precisely behind the last man." The effect of the gesture was instantaneous. "Never again did I witness such a concerted leap forward as at that second," wrote Meyer. "As if bitten by tarantulas, we dive around the rock spur and into a fresh crater." In the end, the pressure from the attackers proved too intense for the embattled Greeks, who broke in a rout. Meyer lost only 6 men killed and 9 wounded; he collected more than 1,000 prisoners.

On the following day, Meyer's detachment captured the town of Kastoria, along with 11,000 Greek prisoners and a wealth of stores and equipment. By April 19 both the Greek and British armies were retreating, and the Germans were in hot pursuit. The swift Leibstandarte was able to outdistance the Greeks and on April 20 blocked their escape by capturing the pass near Metsovon. Late that afternoon, the divisions of the Greek Epirus-Macedonian Army surrendered to Sepp Dietrich, who treated them magnanimously. For their part, in what can only have been an incongruous scene, the defeated Greek forces saluted their conquerors with cries of

"Heil Hitler!" and "Heil Germania!" Three days later at Salonika, in Macedonia, the rest of the Greek army laid down its arms; the British troops by then were fleeing the country by sea.

With his southern flank endangered no more, Adolf Hitler belatedly turned full attention to Operation Barbarossa, his grandiose scheme for the conquest of Russia. And at dawn on June 22, 1941, the Führer unleashed his juggernaut in the largest land attack in the history of warfare. More than three million German soldiers—formed into three army groups—had taken positions along a front 900 miles long, from the Baltic in the north to the Black Sea in the south, and were poised to thrust deep into Soviet territory in sweeping salients. Field Marshal Ritter von Leeb's Army Group North, with the SS Totenkopf and SS Polizei divisions attached, was to push through the Baltic States toward the city of Leningrad; Army Group Center, under the command of Field Marshal Fedor von Bock, would press forward in the direction of Moscow with the SS division Reich; and Field Marshal Gerd von Rundstedt's Army Group South, accompanied by the SS division Wiking and the heavily reinforced Leibstandarte Adolf Hitler, would advance through the Ukraine to Kiev.

The invasion unfolded with resounding success. General Franz Halder, chief of the general staff of the German army, recorded in his diary on June 22 that the Soviet armed forces were "tactically surprised along the entire front." A few days later an ebullient Halder confided to his journal

Buildings blaze as troops of the SS division Reich cross a road in Russia during the opening of Operation Barbarossa in the summer of 1941. Advancing near the center of the German line, they fought to within a few miles of Moscow before the December snows and Russian resistance checked the assault.

that the Red Army would be completely defeated in a matter of weeks.

By July 16 German armor under General Guderian had rolled into Smolensk, only 200 miles from Moscow, and Halder's prophecy seemed to be coming true. Hitler, too, was ecstatic at the prospect of an early victory. "We have only to kick in the door," he told General Alfred Jodl, his OKW chief of staff, "and the whole rotten structure will come crashing down." And everywhere the German forces were kicking with great effect; by the end of September Kiev and 665,000 Soviet prisoners had fallen into German hands, as had the breadbasket of the Ukraine. Leningrad was under attack, and soon Moscow would be imperiled.

Then came the *Rasputitza*, the season of mud. Autumn rains turned the Russian roads into quagmires and slowed the rolling German advance to a sticky crawl. Worse, the merciless Russian winter was only weeks away, and the Germans were ill-prepared to cope with the brutal cold. In the south, the news was bad. The Red Army succeeded in dislodging its enemy, including the Leibstandarte, from Rostov; it was Germany's first major setback on the Eastern Front.

On December 1 Hitler launched an all-out assault on Moscow. After coming within sight of the city's spires and cupolas, however, the German charge was brought to a stop by the combination of furious Soviet resistance and sub-zero temperatures. Then, on December 6, the Red Army

In August 1941 Waffen-SS troops prevail on a Russian civilian to translate a captured banner that urges the followers of Lenin and Stalin to defend communism. Disillusioned with Soviet rule, many in the Ukraine welcomed the Germans as liberators, but others held out fiercely against the occupying force.

lashed out in a murderous counterattack, driving the Germans back forty miles. By the end of the year, as the Russians continued to hammer away at the Nazi war machine, one of every four German soldiers on the Eastern Front had lost his life or been wounded, and a chastened General Halder admitted on the pages of his chronicle that "the myth of the invincibility of the German army was broken."

In the midst of hard going, the Waffen-SS was garnering more praise from the Wehrmacht. Writing to Himmler as the Germans were being pushed back from Moscow, General Eberhard von Mackensen, commander of the III Panzer Corps, assured the SS chief "that the Leibstandarte enjoys an outstanding reputation not only with its superiors but also among its army comrades." Mackensen went on to commend the Leibstandarte for "its inner discipline, its cool daredeviltry, its cheerful enterprise, its unshakable firmness in a crisis, its exemplary toughness, its camaraderie." Even an enemy, a captured Russian officer, offered words of high praise for the Waffen-SS, specifically the Wiking Division, which he described as possessing greater resolve than any other German or Soviet unit. The Russians, he said, breathed a sigh of gratitude when the Wiking was relieved for a time by regular-army units.

But there was a dark side to the way some Waffen-SS units waged war that troubled not only Wehrmacht commanders but officers of the SS itself. Along with the extraordinary spirit and the reckless courage of the SS fighting men ran the strain of cruelty that the Totenkopf troops had displayed earlier in the war when they gunned down British prisoners in France. Many incidents were recorded in which members of the Waffen-SS shot Russian stragglers and prisoners of war. In the Ukraine—where people had at first welcomed the Germans as their liberators from the Bolsheviks—Waffen-SS soldiers dealt savagely with civilians, raping and murdering them. Although a number of these crimes were committed in reprisal for equally barbaric acts perpetrated by Russian troops, many Germans who were in the army or at home and were aware of the misdeeds found them repugnant and disheartening.

The reckless disregard for their own lives cost the Waffen-SS troops a terrible toll of casualties. By late October 1941 the combat effectiveness of the Leibstandarte had been halved by dysentery and combat casualties. The division Reich, now formally designated Das Reich, had lost 60 percent of its strength even before joining the assault on the city of Moscow and being mauled in the subsequent Russian counteroffensive. By February of 1942 one of its regiments, Der Führer, was able to muster only 35 of its original 2,000 men, and the Waffen-SS as a whole had suffered 43,000 casualties. In the months ahead heavy losses would only make the lists

Young Ukrainian women attend a local festival with escorts from the Waffen-SS in July 1942. Such mingling already was waning in occupied Russia as SS leaders urged their troops to scorn the Slavic *Untermenschen*, or subhumans, and the Ukranians, in turn, learned to fear the occupiers they once embraced.

grow longer; by 1943 fully one-third of the Waffen-SS troops originally committed to Operation Barbarossa were dead, missing, or wounded.

The increasingly costly butcher's bill presented by the Russian campaign gave crucial impetus to Gottlob Berger's recruiting efforts at home. While continuing to recruit "racially pure" volunteers from the conquered countries of western and northern Europe, Berger now sought ethnic Germans in such eastern countries as Yugoslavia, Rumania, and Hungary. At first he did not find it difficult to attract foreign recruits. The reputation of the Waffen-SS as the elite of the German armed forces, or just the glamorous appeal of its uniform, provided sufficient bait. Some men enlisted to satisfy a yearning for adventure. Others signed up simply to eat better food. Still

A sniper with the division Das Reich becomes a shock of grain in an inventive, if uncomfortable, bit of camouflage concocted on the Russian steppes in the summer of 1942.

others were politically motivated; for them, service in the SS offered the hope, however misguided, that a German victory would save their nations from the yoke of Bolshevism.

Whatever their reasons, all of these foreigners became fodder for an SS sorely in need of men, and Himmler and Berger were more than happy to nurture any of their illusions. The SS was able to cast its net even wider after Hitler approved the formation of *freiwilligen Legionen,* or volunteer legions, that would accept foreign recruits who fell short of the usual SS racial standards. By the end of August 1941 four such national legions—Danish, Dutch, Flemish, and Norwegian—had been raised for the "battle against Bolshevism." Initially, their members were not considered SS men as such, although they served under SS regulations and drew SS pay. However, by the end of 1942, these legions on Hitler's orders had been fully incorporated into the Waffen-SS.

Inevitably, as German battlefield fortunes turned downward and Waffen-SS troops were devoured by the thousands in the great maw of the Russian campaign, volunteers became hard to find. Berger's SS recruiters resorted to ever more dubious means of refilling the ranks. Members of the Reich's Labor Corps were conscripted without choice, and the boys of the Hitler Youth organization were intimidated into volunteering. Press gangs rounded up ethnic Germans for service. Lieutenant General Hans Jüttner, head of the SS high command, complained as early as 1942 that many so-called volunteers had actually been lured into the Waffen-SS through trickery; he cited the case of Hungarian nationals who joined up thinking they were going off for "short sports training." Worse, the recruiters tended to take anyone they could get, regardless of qualifications. According to Jüttner, some of the recruits were suffering from "epilepsy, severe tuberculosis, and other serious physical disabilities."

Such complaints, even when they came from so high a source, mattered little to Gottlob Berger. The SS urgently needed soldiers; that stark necessity took precedence over any general's scruples—and ultimately over Himmler's reservations about racial purity. By August 1942, in fact, Himmler had convinced himself that natives of Soviet Estonia were racially indistinguishable from Germans and could therefore form an Estonian Legion within the framework of the Waffen-SS. This crack in the armor of SS racial purity could only widen as casualties mounted and the shortage of troops deepened. Eventually, the ranks of the SS were filled with even Himmler's despised Slavic *Unter-*

A hooded and masked SS soldier in Russia uses binoculars during the winter of 1942-1943. After their fearful experiences the previous year, the Germans were now better equipped to withstand "General Winter."

A dead SS driver exemplifies the fate of more than 100,000 Waffen-SS recruits who fell in Russia by mid-1943. "We weren't outfought," wrote Kurt Meyer, "but we were outnumbered, overwhelmed, pushed to the wall by sheer weight."

menschen, or subhumans—with entire units composed of Soviet Cossacks and Ukrainians and even Yugoslav Muslims—until by the end of the war fully half of the SS divisions consisted mostly of foreigners.

The Waffen-SS grew phenomenally throughout the remaining years of the war. At the beginning of 1943 it numbered more than 200,000 men; a year later it had doubled in size, and there were six SS army corps. Before the fighting ended, a total of thirty-eight divisions, organized into nine army corps, had seen action beneath the banner of the Waffen-SS.

Yet few, if any, of the divisions assembled in the later years of the war resembled the original Waffen-SS in anything but name. Wholesale and indiscriminant recruiting, combined with demoralizing defeats in the field and escalating casualties, had changed the character of the Waffen-SS. Few of the replacements were infected by the Nazi fanaticism that inspired the original members of the Waffen-SS to acts of reckless bravery and suicidal determination in the name of Adolf Hitler. Foreigners and unwilling conscripts rarely performed with the élan of their predecessors. Gradually, the Waffen-SS lost much, but never all, of its elite flair.

The original Waffen-SS units, however, continued to fight with fanatical fervor. Those units—the Leibstandarte Adolf Hitler, Das Reich, and the Totenkopf Division—had been so battered by the Russian winter counteroffensive of 1941-1942 that they were pulled out of line and sent to France, where they were refitted and reinforced as *Panzergrenadier*, or armored infantry divisions. Later they were given additional tanks and formed into the II SS Panzer Corps—a phalanx of steel on which Hitler was counting to reverse his flagging fortunes on the Eastern Front. There, in early February 1943, the battle for the strategic city of Stalingrad had ended in a devastating German defeat. Three hundred thousand German troops had been killed or captured. To make up for this demoralizing loss and to halt the Soviets' latest winter offensive, Hitler had ordered a vigorous counterattack aimed at the industrial city of Kharkov.

In the vanguard of the attack were the three armored divisions of the new II SS Panzer Corps, under the command of Lieutenant General Paul Hausser. It would be, perhaps, their finest hour.

When the order to attack came on February 19, Hausser and his Waffen-SS troops were sixty miles southwest of the city—and in retreat. Three days earlier, the panzer divisions had been engulfed by the Russian tide sweeping around Kharkov. Hitler ordered Hausser to stand fast and fight to the death, but the crusty, confident panzer leader considered the directive to be senseless; instead, he and his troops broke out of the city. Now Hausser reversed field, went on the attack, and slammed into the Soviet Sixth Army.

173

With support from the Luftwaffe and other armored units, Hausser's panzers were able to break through the Russians with only light casualties and again bear down on Kharkov, skirmishing with enemy tanks in village after village as they went.

Reaching Kharkov on March 9, Hausser sent the Leibstandarte plunging ahead. In less than a day of fierce house-to-house fighting, Dietrich's division knifed to the center of the city. Das Reich and Totenkopf, meanwhile, laid a snare around Kharkov, trapping the Soviet defenders inside. By March 15 the men of the Leibstandarte had mopped up the last pockets of resistance, and Kharkov once again belonged to the Waffen-SS. Moreover, the victory succeeded in stopping the Russian offensive and stabilized the front. Hitler was ecstatic because his faith in the SS panzer corps had been validated. And the Reich now had a fresh chance to gain the upper hand on the Eastern Front.

Heinrich Himmler, too, brimmed with pride. He visited Hausser's victorious troops in Kharkov and urged them to greater deeds with a rousing speech: "We will never let fade that excellent weapon, the dread and terrible reputation that preceded us in the battles for Kharkov, but will constantly add meaning to it."

The generals and the fighting men had no way of knowing it at the time, but Hausser and the Waffen-SS had just won the last great German victory of the war. The fortunes of battle were about to swing irrevocably to the Russians, whose next great counteroffensive would not stop until it reached Berlin. The Waffen-SS would fight other battles to stave off the end of nazism—ultimately in vain. As a fighting force it had peaked at Kharkov. In no more than two years it would go down in final defeat, along with the fanatical dreamers who created it. ✚

The Pride of "the Führer's Own"

"In the Leibstandarte we think ourselves a cut above the rest," a member of that Waffen-SS unit wrote home on the eve of the invasion of Russia. "We are the only ones! The Führer's own to do with as he will!" Such proud fealty to Hitler was the birthright of the Leibstandarte, which had originated as the Führer's personal bodyguard. Its men alone wore his name on the cuff of their uniform sleeve and proclaimed it atop their flagstaff *(left)*. Indeed, the Leibstandarte was Hitler's alter ego in the field, and its career mirrored his own.

Beginning as a headquarters detachment that was more show than substance, it evolved into a ruthlessly efficient fighting force, only to face a bitter reckoning at the war's end.

The Leibstandarte was conceived in 1933 when Hitler loyalist Sepp Dietrich selected 120 SS men to watch over the Führer. Early on, the guards spent much of their time on parade or serving as waiters and musicians. They earned notoriety as executioners during the Blood Purge of 1934, but to regular-army men they remained "asphalt soldiers"—daunting only at drill. In time, however, officer-graduates of the SS Junker schools worked the Leibstandarte into fighting trim. As a motorized infantry regiment leading the push into Holland in 1940, it advanced 105 miles in a single day. Later the Leibstandarte managed similar feats in Russia, where it was built into a full armored division. But its reputation was sullied by persistent reports that its men shot prisoners in cold blood; in one infamous episode in 1944, more than seventy Americans were killed after they had surrendered. General Dietrich would answer to the victorious Allies for that deed, but before the day of judgment, his far-ranging division would be denounced by its own overlord. Early in 1945, upon learning that the Leibstandarte had withdrawn after failing to stop the Russians in Hungary, Hitler wildly accused the men of treachery and ordered them to remove the cuff bands bearing his name—a command that Dietrich, defying the SS imperative, refused to obey.

Tame Beginnings as a Household Guard

Members of the Leibstandarte guard the entrance to the new Reich Chancellery, Hitler's palatial Berlin headquarters, completed in January 1939. To set the proper tone, Hitler had the guards stand vigil in their parade uniforms, complete with white gloves and belts.

Celebration of Hitler's birthday on April 20, a national holiday, meant extra duties for the Leibstandarte. At top, aproned orderlies deliver a birthday cake garnished with a swastika to the dining hall of the old Reich Chancellery; at left, security men sift through presents sent to the Führer and intercept anything harmful or derogatory.

This dance band was part of the Leibstandarte's Music Corps, which also played at the 1936 Olympic Games.

On January 30, 1938, an anniversary of Nazi rule, Hitler *(left)* hails his parading Leibstandarte, now 3,000 strong, on Berlin's

Wilhelmstrasse. Six weeks later, elements of the regiment marched into Vienna to cement Austria's annexation.

Troops of the Leibstandarte, now a panzer division fighting in Russia, pull back from the battle at Kursk in July 1943. In the last days of the battle—a crushing setback for the Germans—Hitler transferred the division to Italy. Mussolini, he explained, needed "elite formations that are politically close to fascism."

Hotly engaged with Polish forces west of Warsaw in September 1939, troops of the 2d Battalion Leibstandarte fire from the shelter of a shattered cart. Rushed into action before their combat training had been completed, members of the Leibstandarte learned painful lessons in Poland: "Fearless attack," their commanding general noted, "was paid for repeatedly with heavy losses."

A Record
Stained by
Atrocities

182

Photographs taken behind German lines in Russia document the capture and summary execution of suspected partisans by members of the Leibstandarte. German soldiers approach a barn with rifles at the ready *(left)*, then flush men in civilian clothes from the building *(center)*, and shoot a captive on the spot *(right)*.

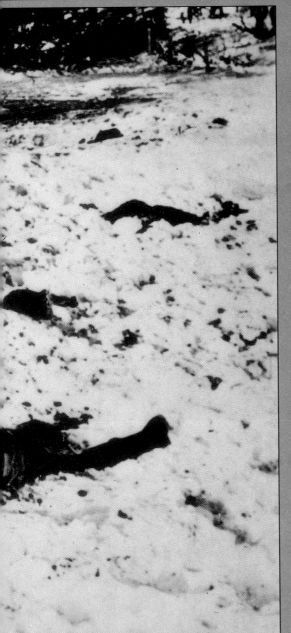

Dead American soldiers lie in the snow at Malmédy, Belgium, where they were machine-gunned after surrendering to troops of the Leibstandarte on December 16, 1944. The bodies were numbered before the photograph was introduced as evidence in the war-crimes trials at Nuremberg that sentenced Sepp Dietrich and several of his subordinates to prison. Similar atrocities earlier in the war prompted criticism of the Leibstandarte within the German high command. But Hitler refused to rein in his cherished unit. "The Leibstandarte," the Führer said, "must be allowed to perform its special tasks in its own way."

A Lowering
of Flags
in Red Square

In June of 1945, the bare staff of
the division that fought under
Hitler's name (*left*) is lowered
along with other captured
German standards to the pave-
ment of Moscow's Red Square.
The cloth banner that hung from
the staff was never found.

Acknowledgments

The editors thank: Belgium: Brussels— Le Centre de Recherches et d'Études de la Seconde Guerre Mondiale; Le Musée Royal de L'Armée et d'Histoire Militaire. Czechoslovakia: Prague—Czechoslovak News Agency. England: London—Terry Charman, Laurie Milner, Imperial War Museum; Andrew Mollo. Surrey—Brian Davis. Federal Republic of Germany: Berlin—Heidi Klein, Bildarchiv Preussischer Kulturbesitz; Gabrielle Kohler-Gallei, Archiv für Kunst und Geschichte; Wolfgang Streubel, Ullstein Bilderdienst. Hamburg—Heinz Höne. Koblenz—Meinrad Nilges, Bundesarchiv. Munich—Elisabeth Heidt, Süddeutscher Verlag Bilderdienst; Heinrich Hoffmann. Osnabrück—Helmuth Thöle, Munin-Verlag. Wuppertal—Jost W. Schneider. German Democratic Republic: Berlin—Hannes Quaschinsky, ADN Zentralbild. Netherlands: Amsterdam—The Dutch State Institute for War Documentation; Karel Ornstein, Saskia van de Linde. United States: California— Thomas W. Pooler. Illinois—William L. Combs, Associate Professor of History, Western Illinois University. Virginia—Ray Embree. Yugoslavia: Belgrade—Pavle Ljumovic, Military Museum. Sarajevo— Dr. Ahmed Hadzirovic, Director, Museum of Revolution of Bosnia and Herzegovina.

Picture Credits

Bibliography

Angolia, John R., *Cloth Insignia of the SS.* San Jose, Calif.: R. James Bender, 1983.

Association of Soldiers of the Former Waffen-SS, *When All Our Brothers Are Silent: The Book of Photographs of the Waffen-SS.* Osnabrück, W.Ger.: Munin-Verlag, 1975.

Bethell, Nicholas, and the Editors of Time-Life Books, *Russia Besieged* (World War II series). Alexandria, Va.: Time-Life Books, 1977.

Bullock, Alan, *Hitler: A Study in Tyranny.* New York: Harper & Row, 1962.

Butler, Rupert, *The Black Angels: The Story of the Waffen-SS.* Middlesex, England: Hamlyn, 1978.

Crankshaw, Edward, *Gestapo: Instrument of Tyranny.* New York: Viking, 1957.

Dallin, Alexander, *German Rule in Russia, 1941-1945.* New York: Octagon Books, 1980.

Deschner, Günther, *Reinhard Heydrich.* New York: Stein and Day, 1981.

Engelmann, Bernt, *In Hitler's Germany.* Transl. by Krishna Winston. New York: Schocken Books, 1986.

Fest, Joachim C., *The Face of the Third Reich.* Transl. by Michael Bullock. New York: Pantheon Books, 1970.

Frischauer, Willi, *Himmler: The Evil Genius of the Third Reich.* London: Odhams, 1953.

Graber, G. S., *History of the SS.* New York: David McKay, 1978.

Grunberger, Richard, *Hitler's SS.* New York: Delacorte, 1970.

Hausser, Paul, *Soldaten Wie Andere Auch: Der Weg der Waffen-SS.* Osnabrück, W.Ger.: Munin-Verlag, 1966.

Henry, Clarissa, and Marc Hillel, *Of Pure Blood.* Transl. by Eric Mossbacher. New York: McGraw-Hill, 1976.

Herzstein, Robert Edwin, and the Editors of Time-Life Books, *The Nazis* (World War II series). Alexandria, Va.: Time-Life Books, 1980.

Hoess, Rudolf, *Commandant of Auschwitz: The Autobiography of Rudolf Hoess.* Transl. by Constantine FitzGibbon. Cleveland: World, 1959.

Hoettl, Wilhelm, *The Secret Front: The Story of Nazi Political Espionage.* New York: Frederick A. Praeger, 1954.

Höhne, Heinz, *The Order of the Death's Head.* Transl. by Richard Barry. New York: Ballantine Books, 1971.

Keegan, John, *Waffen SS: The Asphalt Soldiers.* New York: Ballantine Books, 1970.

Koehl, Robert Lewis:
The Black Corps. Madison: University of Wisconsin Press, 1983.
RKFDV: German Resettlement and Population Policy, 1939-1945. Cambridge, Mass.: Harvard University Press, 1957.

Kogon, Eugen, *The Theory and Practice of Hell: The German Concentration Camps and the System behind Them.* Transl. by Heinz Norden. New York: Berkley Books, 1980.

Komjathy, Anthony Tihamer, and Rebecca Stockwell, *German Minorities and the Third Reich.* New York: Holmes & Meier, 1980.

Krausnick, Helmut, et al., *Anatomy of the SS State.* Transl. by Richard Barry, Marian Jackson, and Dorothy Long. New York: Walker, 1968.

Lefèvre, Eric, "La SS-Tarnjacke: La Blouse de Toile Bariolée de la Waffen-SS (1937-1944)." *Militaria,* June/July 1986.

Lehmann, Rudolf, *Die Leibstandarte im Bild.* Osnabrück, W.Ger.: Munin-Verlag, 1988.

Manvell, Roger, *SS and Gestapo: Rule by Terror.* New York: Ballantine Books, 1969.

Manvell, Roger, and Heinrich Fraenkel, *Himmler.* New York: G. P. Putnam's Sons, 1965.

Marrus, Michael R., *The Unwanted: European Refugees in the Twentieth Century.* New York: Oxford University Press, 1985.

Mollo, Andrew:
A Pictorial History of the SS, 1923-1945. New York: Bonanza Books, 1979.
To the Death's Head True. London: Thames Methuen, 1982.

Quarrie, Bruce:
Hitler's Samurai: The Waffen-SS in Action. New York: Arco, 1983.
Hitler's Teutonic Knights: SS Panzers in Action. Wellingborough, England: Patrick Stephens, 1986.

Reitlinger, Gerald, *The SS: Alibi of a Nation, 1922-1945.* London: Arms and Armour, 1981.

Rutherford, Ward, *Hitler's Propaganda Machine.* London: Bison Books, 1978.

Schneider, Jost W., *Their Honor Was Loyalty.* Ed. and transl. by Winder McConnell. San Jose, Calif.: R. James Bender, 1977.

Schulze-Kossens, R., *Officer Training in the Waffen-SS: The Junkerschools.* Osnabrück, W.Ger.: Munin-Verlag, 1987.

Smith, Bradley F., and Agnes F. Peterson, eds., *Heinrich Himmler: Geheimreden 1933 bis 1945 und Andere Ansprachen.* Frankfurt: Propyläen Verlag, 1974.

Stein, George H., *The Waffen SS: Hitler's Elite Guard at War, 1939-1945.* Ithaca, N.Y.: Cornell University Press, 1966.

Stumpp, Karl, *The German-Russians: Two Centuries of Pioneering.* Bonn: Edition Atlantic-Forum, 1967.

Sydnor, Charles W., Jr., *Soldiers of Destruction: The SS Death's Head Division, 1933-1945.* Princeton, N.J.: Princeton University Press, 1977.

Taylor, Telford, *The March of Conquest: The German Victories in Western Europe, 1940.* New York: Simon and Schuster, 1958.

Wegner, Bernd, *Hitlers Politische Soldaten: Die Waffen-SS, 1933-1945.* Paderborn, W.Ger.: Ferdinand Schöningh, 1983.

Weingartner, James J., *Hitler's Guard: The Story of the Leibstandarte SS Adolf Hitler, 1933-1945.* Carbondale, Ill.: Southern Illinois University Press, 1974.

Wiesenthal, Simon, *Every Day Remembrance Day: A Chronicle of Jewish Martyrdom.* New York: Henry Holt, 1987.

Wykes, Alan, *SS Leibstandarte.* New York: Ballantine Books, 1974.

Index

Time-Life Books Inc. offers a wide range of fine recordings, including a *Rock 'n' Roll Era* series. For subscription information, call 1-800-621-7026 or write Time-Life Music, P.O. Box C-32068, Richmond, Virginia 23261-2068.